KIERKEGAARD

A *Brief Overview*
of the Life and Writings of
Søren Kierkegaard

1813-1855

ALBERT ANDERSON

Lutheran University Press
Minneapolis, Minnesota

KIERKEGAARD
A Brief Overview of the
Life and Writings of Søren Kierkegaard
1813-1855
by Albert Anderson

Copyright © 2010 Lutheran University Press, an imprint of 1517 Media. All rights reserved. No part of this publication may be reproduced, stored in a retrieval system, or transmitted in any form or by any means, electronic, mechanical, photocopying, recording, or otherwise, without written permission of the publisher: 1517 Media Permissions, PO BOX 1209, Minneapolis, MN 55440-1209 or copyright@1517.media.

Library of Congress Cataloging-In-Publication Data

Anderson, Albert, 1928-
  Kierkegaard : a brief overview of the life and writings of Søren Kierkegaard, 1813-1855 / Albert Anderson.
     p. cm.
  Includes index.
  ISBN-13: 978-1-932688-53-5 (alk. paper)
  ISBN-10: 1-932688-53-6 (alk. paper)
  eISBN: 978-1-942304-62-3
  1. Kierkegaard, Søren, 1813-1855. I. Title.

  B4377.A573 2010
  198'.9—dc22
  [B]
                                            2010030333

Kirk House Publishers, PO Box 390759, Minneapolis, MN 55439
Manufactured in the United States of America

CONTENTS

Dedication 5
Foreword 7
Preface 9
Early Development 12
Authorship 20
Stages 27
Despair 38
Self 45
Subjectivity 50
Religiousness 60
Discourse 69
Change 75
Conflict 86
Postscript 89
Afterthoughts 93
Acknowledgments 97
Pertinent Dates and Facts about Kierkegaard 98
Chronology of Relevent Historical Figures 101
Index 104

"Kierkegaard as a University Student" by Jacobson
Print from the collection of the author

DEDICATION

To Reidar Thomte, Paul Holmer, and Krister Stendahl,
memorable mentors;
and to David and Lillian Swenson,
and Howard and Edna Hong,
whose legacies of
commentary and translation
of Kierkegaard
are for the ages.

FOREWORD

Understanding the great nineteenth century Danish theologian, philosopher, and psychologist, Søren Kierkegaard, and appropriating his insights is not easy. Yet Kierkegaard's insights to the understanding of human existence ought to be widely shared. This primer is not designed as a contribution to advanced Kierkegaard studies. Instead it provides a reliable point of departure for pastors, teachers, students, leaders in congregations and institutions, as well as the general reading public. Great numbers of people have heard of Kierkegaard but have not had opportunity to discover the nature of his contribution. This book helps fill that gap and could be used as a supplemental text, discussion/study piece, or simply as an inviting, challenging read.

There is no easy way to plumb the depths of Søren Kierkegaard and his work. The average person is going to need help in understanding Kierkegaard's life and work. Yet his contribution to human understanding and action deserves close attention for anyone seeking to know what it means to be an existing person. Kierkegaard does not present a philosophical system to explain existence. On the contrary, he vigorously opposes philosophical system builders. Kierkegaard's express intent is to engage the individual person and create opportunities for self-understanding and purposeful personal action.

In this work Kierkegaard's key themes are identified and briefly described. The reader is given a taste of Kierkegaard's primary concerns and given opportunity to see how his writings elucidate those concerns. Thought processes are stimulated, for Kierkegaard deals with the basic stuff of life in a challenging way. His technique of the writing as well as the substance requires help. The fact that Kierkegaard uses two very different bodies of writing calls for an introductory explanation. There is a large body of work that is written pseudonymously under a variety of pen names. Another body, largely sermons, bears Kierkegaard's name as author and expresses his personal faith. Without advance acquaintance of this technique, it would be very difficult for the casual reader to understand Kierkegaard.

Kierkegaard had harsh words for the Christian church as an institution, especially as it existed in the Danish state church of his day. One of his books is entitled *Attack on Christendom*. It is important to know that "Christendom" is attacked, not Christianity. Kierkegaard wants no part of "cheap grace." He provides a serious warning for all circumstances in which people are assumed to be "Christian" because they are born into a particular ethnic group or nation.

Kierkegaard's books will not disappear. He deals with timeless themes. What does it mean to be a "self"? What does it mean to make a "leap" of faith? How does one deal with despair, angst, dread? How does one discover oneself on the esthetic, moral, and religious planes of life? To what is Kierkegaard pointing when he declares that "truth is subjectivity"? Such questions will not go away. Humans will always be struggling with them.

Kierkegaard's work is many-faceted and often difficult. A small group joining in the reading and discussing this book will provide a fascinating experience.

David W. Preus

PREFACE

For those who are curious about the life and work of Søren Kierkegaard, the nineteenth century Danish philosopher-theologian, but who may be apprehensive of the scholarly books devoted to his often complex thought and thus feel ill-equipped to understand him, I offer in what follows a brief overview—not, perhaps, a conventional introduction, but a small book that I trust will be neither intimidating nor condescending, yet worthy of the subject.

True, Kierkegaard is wonderfully challenging and, given the great admiration I have for the legendary scholarship of interpreters like David F. Swenson, Walter Lowrie, Paul Holmer, Nils Thulstrup, Reidar Thomte, Howard and Edna Hong, and many others, what follows is but a footnote—though not, I believe, without credibility of its own. Works interpreting Søren Kierkegaard, many now out of print though found in some libraries, have been available in various languages for several decades. For example, with a brilliant introduction from Professor Swenson, one of the best is a collection of lectures given by Eduard Geismar in the late thirties, an overview that virtually introduced Kierkegaard to American readers. Then there is *Kierkegaard's Philosophy of Religion* by Reidar Thomte, Princeton University Press, 1949, a fine piece of work from which I and countless other students over the years first learned about Søren Kierkegaard. Occasionally I will cite their work or my notes when the source is evident.

Indeed, as the result of so many years in the company of Kierkegaard and his interpreters, I hardly recognize my own reflections from those of others. For the reader, that is an advantage, though for my purposes—and with profound apologies to those on whom I rely—I choose a form with few specific credits.

While I am capable of translating Søren Kierkegaard's work from the Danish in which he wrote, I am not likely to improve on current versions, especially the outstanding efforts of Howard and Edna Hong, whose introductory notes and a fine compilation of excerpts from the complete translation of *Kierkegaard's Writings* are found in their more recent work, *The Essential Kierkegaard,* Postscript, Inc. 1995, 1997, 1998, 2000; Princeton University Press, 1978, 1980; Julia Watkin, 1990; Todd W. Nichol, 1997. In that respect I am greatly indebted to the Hongs and others. I rely substantially on the *Writings* and the excerpts for passages I use in an attempt nonetheless to offer a modest reading that with obvious limitations may still serve to introduce Søren Kierkegaard to a wider public.

From the interest that continues to be shown in Kierkegaard's writings decade after decade throughout the world, their relevance to generation after generation is amazing. Countless students old and young still learn from Kierkegaard's work even after many readings. Why, I have often wondered, is this so? Following a lecture I once gave on the theme of despair to which Kierkegaard speaks so eloquently, I asked a young girl why she was apparently so taken with the idea. All she said was "We know despair." Again, to the uninitiated in matters of philosophy, theology, or classical literature, Kierkegaard's frequent allusions to them may seem daunting, though in what follows most are understood in context while some invite further study. What is important to know is that Kierkegaard wrote for "that solitary individual, the reader I call my own"—ordinary people, not really the learned scholars of northern Europe or even just the citizens of Copenhagen. He wrote for every thoughtful reader everywhere in every time. How, you may ask, could one be so bold as to presume this? One reason: The self in its multiple dimensions, coupled with the human condition—existence—to which he gave his remarkable thought and passion, are universal, timeless, and about which we are incessantly preoccupied. And no author does a better job of plumbing their mysterious depths. That is why he can be understood and why he should be read.

Would Søren Kierkegaard have approved of this modest effort? Probably not, unless he hoped it would lead the reader into the complete works. He did admit—without apology—they would be difficult to understand; but with that, he simply left it to the reader to divine what he had in mind. Warning aside, we who read and write about him must presume to understand and interpret him rightly or wrongly—and without apology. A lengthy conversation with him would help, of course. Barring that, I trust that what follows is more helpful than misleading, more lucid than cloudy. If so, I would expect readers to better understand Søren Kierkegaard and to decide which of his works they wish to read first.

EARLY DEVELOPMENT

It is clear from his early journals and letters, prior to the authorship he ultimately developed, that Søren Kierkegaard was a precocious, broadly educated student. Even in his early twenties as well as throughout his authorship, his works are peppered with allusions and analogies. One author (Thomas Oden, *The Parables of Kierkegaard*, Princeton University Press, 1978) has collected an entire book of his "parables"— gleaned from dozens of ancient and contemporary historians, statesmen, philosophers, theologians, scientists, poets, playwrights, and novelists.

Born on May 5, 1813, in the city of Copenhagen, Denmark, Søren Aabye was the youngest of seven children and of a second marriage. "Born old," he said of himself, not least because his father, Michael Pederson, was already fifty-seven and retired; born in a country whose citizens by birth were nominal Lutherans, about which Kierkegaard once slyly remarked that while New Testament Christianity required that a person be born a second time, Danish Christianity required only that a person be born.

Very likely Kierkegaard's uncommon thirst for knowledge was in large part instilled in him by his father who, devoted to learning late in life and who had the liberty to do so following a successful business career, took special pains to educate Søren himself. The nature of this home schooling was drawn in part from the ancients, especially the classics such as the well-known *Dialogues of Plato* in which the legendary Socrates (469-399 B.C.), Plato's teacher in Athens, Greece, is depicted as an obstinately curious conversationalist notorious for challenging and questioning the unexamined opinions of persons he met. In that manner he revealed the contradictions which prominent citizens were forced to admit about their ideas of piety, knowledge, bravery, love, and the like.

For example, Socrates, in the Platonic dialogue *Euthyphro*, by chance engages a citizen of Athens, Euthyphro, in a discussion to know why he is about to prosecute his own father who apparently has been found guilty of murder. Euthyphro responds that murder is an act of impiety and he is only doing what the gods would want, what is pleasing to them. Socrates reminds him that the gods are known to disagree about moral questions; still, if they agree, do the gods love piety because it is pious, or is it pious because the gods love it? OK, Euthyphro says, let us say piety is the just thing to do. Then, after Socrates has challenged the narrowness of the view, Euthyphro agrees that the concept of justice applies in part to gods and in part to man. But Socrates wants to know why it should apply to the gods at all; it is of no benefit to them, but only a service we seem to accord them. Finally, Euthyphro suggests that piety amounts to the words and actions acceptable to the gods. As Plato, the author, puts it in the dialogue, Socrates challenges Euthyphro to explain piety not by recourse to examples of what people call pious actions, but by concern for a clear definition, one that rationally reveals the universal "ideal" or essence which all so-called pious actions have in common. As we shall note later, an idea-like reality is Plato's view, not that of the historical Socrates.

So too, Søren's father regularly challenged the youthful boy's readings and beliefs, engaging him forcefully in Socratic-like dialogue. This kind of tutoring left Søren with a profound devotion to Socrates and the ancients, and led him to develop a unique writing style of his own: "dialectical" (related to dialogue), a relentless kind of self-conscious reflection and argument, a dramatic dialogue or debate with himself or imagined others. But more of this later.

There is another reason his father gave special attention to Søren's education. The son of a sheepherder, Søren's father spent his youth among the desolate dunes and heaths of Jutland, the province northwest of Copenhagen. In time he moved to the city where he ultimately became a prosperous hosiery merchant. Still, his childhood experiences as a young herder affected him deeply, particularly the memory of a time alone with the sheep when in great despair he cursed God for condemning him to such a miserable life.

Reminiscent of the Old Testament story of Abraham (a story Kierkegaard would later use), it was a curse he felt he could atone for only by offering his youngest son, his sacrificial Isaac, to God. So he determined to give Søren the best possible education that would also prepare him for a ministerial career in the Lutheran Church of Denmark. Growing up in a household in which piety was uppermost and the rules for moral behavior strict, it is not strange that once Søren gained his freedom to attend the university, he resisted—with the gusto of youth—his father's intended atonement.

During this period he apparently hung out with like-minded students at popular spots around town. The experience is amply reflected in early works that describe (by one or more of his assumed characters) a rather purposeless life devoted to immediate pleasures and a wayward sense of the future. In real life he was deeply confused about what he should do in life, not least because he realized he could be successful in any one of several careers, for example as a lawyer or an actor.

In fact, since his interests and resources (his father's money) were so extensive, he spent almost ten years in this mode. As it turned out, however, it was hardly a waste of time. For example, late in his years at the university he wrote and successfully defended a doctoral-level thesis, *The Concept of Irony, With Continual Reference to Socrates (1841)*. It develops in scholarly detail the idea of irony as found in well-known German thinkers whose writings and lectures were currently prominent; Kierkegaard attended some of the latter in Berlin. The thesis clearly favors the ironic figure of his classical mentor, Socrates, and becomes a significant resource in his subsequent authorship, as we shall see. Indeed, the influence of the Socratic figure on his life and writings is so central even at this young age that *The Concept of Irony* warrants some attention here. It is a technically difficult work, not for the faint of heart.

At the outset Kierkegaard notes some of the differences in the way certain ancients interpret Socrates' significance. To Kierkegaard, Plato has tried to make Socrates into his own image, something of a speculative idealist searching for a reality that transcends the existing world. Xenophon, a somewhat unreliable Greek historian, sees Socrates as an apostle of the established order, someone of value to society in its aspirations to be a great nation. Others such as the famous comic dramatist, Aristophanes (more later), tends naturally to focus on Socrates' eccentricities, depicting him reclining thoughtfully on a cloud, above it all—a caricaturing, by the way, that Socrates applauded!

None, Kierkegaard says, has captured the real Socrates, whose existence is wholly ironic. He may be sympathetic to the Platonic search for the ideal, but he recognizes it is beyond him, a speculative mystery. He certainly operates in an everyday empirical world, but that is not his focus. He dwells somewhere between the ideal and the ordinary, and yet his work among men, his efforts to clarify and correct common notions, has universal validity. Above all, Socrates epitomizes irony, an element of "subjectivity," one's inwardness, the human self. His existence marks irony's entry into world history for the first time. In fact, Kierkegaard suggests, it represents an event comparable to the impact and intellectual transformation of modern thought brought about by the great eighteenth century German philosopher, Immanuel Kant, whose work in ethics and theory of knowledge was likened to the Copernican Revolution! We will say more about Kant later.

Kierkegaard also notes the interest in irony among his contemporaries, especially that of G. W. F. Hegel, by far the most famous speculative German philosopher of the time. We will have much more to say about Hegel later on. Suffice it to say that Søren Kierkegaard, in *The Concept of Irony*, expresses great disappointment in Hegel's assessment of Socrates, which contended that the latter was, in effect, dishonest in his legendary profession of ignorance, adopting the pose in order to avoid the potential weakness of Socrates' actual views. Søren Kierkegaard credits Hegel for his monumental speculative work, but argues that he is totally wrong about Socrates. The truth, he insists, is that Socrates is genuine in proclaiming his ignorance, sees the futility of speculation (like that of Hegel) for getting at reality, and wants above all to understand himself. If his questioning with its oblique sense of indirection serves to enlighten others in similar fashion, that is the way with irony. So much for Kierkegaard's early devotion to Socrates and its lifelong importance.

Some years earlier, however, he had written in his journal some thoughts that were anything but academic:

> What I really need is to get clear about *what I am to do*, not what I must know, except insofar as knowledge must precede every act. What matters is to find my purpose, to see what it really is that God wills that I shall do; the crucial thing is to find a truth that is truth *for me*, to find *the idea for which I am willing to live and die*. Of what use would it be to me to discover a so-called objective truth, to work through the philosophical systems so that I could, if

asked, make critical judgments about them . . . of what use would it be to me to be able to develop a theory of the state constructing a world I did not live in but merely held up for others to see; of what use would it be to me to be able to formulate the meaning of Christianity—if it had no deeper meaning *for me and for my life?* . . . I certainly do not deny that I still accept *an imperative of knowledge and that through it men may be influenced, but then it must come alive in me,* and *this* is what I now recognize as the most important of all. This is what is lacking, and this is why I am like a man who has collected furniture, rented an apartment, but as yet has not found the beloved to share life's ups and downs with him. It is this inward action of a person, this Godside of a person, that is decisive" (*The Essential Kierkegaard* [hereafter, *TEK*], op. cit., ed. Howard and Edna Hong, p. 8f.).

Thus did the young Kierkegaard begin to sense the challenge which lay before him. Not just a matter of career, though that was difficult enough to decide; it was also the challenge he learned first from Socrates who determined to forego contemporary speculation about the universe in order rather to examine the human self—to know oneself, the truth about one's nature and capacities, before anything else. It meant looking inward, deeply and honestly, to question and clarify what personal existence is all about, and what it really means to exist.

The decisive turn of mind came about in the context of two personal crises—ironically, experiences that also propelled him into one of the most prolific and profound authorships devised in recent times.

The first crisis, the death of his father, occurred when Kierkegaard was twenty-five. At the time, he was actually studying theology in obedience to his dying father's wish. He came to believe that his life would be short, that he would not reach the age of thirty-five, and that God had a singular task for him before that occurred. This sense was deeply troubling for him, one that never left him, and that impelled him to write with uncommon intensity.

It was also emotionally wrenching, complicated—the second crisis—by the fact that he fell in love with a beautiful young girl, Regine Olson, the daughter of a well-known Danish official and several years younger than he. In 1840, three years after their first meeting, he proposed marriage. About a year later, as his forebodings deepened, he abruptly broke off the engagement.

Both he and Regine suffered greatly over the affair. He wrote about it in his journal, regretting that it was a cruel act even though he truly loved her. Still, he felt that God, as he said, had "lodged a veto" against the marriage, and he reflected that his choice was either to throw himself into the most carefree way of life or else to devote himself wholly to a religious career—but one that would be quite different from the conventional requirements of a preacher.

To engage and attempt to overcome his grief with purposeful activity in the months that followed, Kierkegaard virtually threw himself into a prodigious, well-focused writing project. Carefully planned, it totally consumed him for the next several years with the publication of work after work—many of which, we can now understand, he dedicated either to his father or to Regine.

Central to all his works are the collisions of life's values and passions that make up the human predicament: the need to decide and to embody one set of values in favor of another—for no reason sufficient to logic and understanding, but accompanied always by the kind of pathos and inner suffering at having to resign one's former love for the sake of something higher, more profound.

As Kierkegaard comes to develop these themes, in wondrously varied ways, meaning in life is characterized as a matter of the predominate attitudes and commitments which govern one's life and outlook. He does so dialectically—a dialogue with the reader, in self-examining ways that identify or dramatically classify personal existence in terms of the several modes, dimensions, or "stages" that to him typify human existence. He carries out this voluminous project over a relatively short period of time, but longer than the thirty-five years he believed he would live. He died at the relatively young age of forty-two, of uncertain causes.

AUTHORSHIP

Søren Kierkegaard's plan was to write no less than two different kinds of authorship: one by what he called his "left hand," that is, pseudonymously, using assumed names of publishers, authors, and characters; and the other with his "right hand," under his own name, in an effort to set his left hand characters and their principal governing attitudes or fundamental views of life apart from his own. The distinction is also important for a style that represents "indirect communication," a way of eliciting from the reader self-acknowledged truths about what it actually means to exist, comparable to the maieutic or "midwifery" manner in which Socrates aided his fellow citizens in giving birth to the truth.

The left-handed group in roughly chronological order included *Either/Or* (1843), a mixed collection of papers and letters said to have been found in a secret compartment of a desk and brought to publication by Victor Eremita (the hermit); *Fear and Trembling* (1843), a recast of the story of Abraham and Isaac, by Johannes de Silentio (the silent one); *Repetition* (1843) by Constantine Constantius, a consulting psychologist; *Philosophical Fragments* (1844) by Johannes Cimacus; *The Concept of Anxiety* (1844) by Vigilius Haufniensus (the watchman of Copenhagen); *Stages on Life's Way* (1845) by Hilarius Bookbinder, an editor; *The Sickness Unto Death* (1849) and *Practice in Christianity* (1850), both by Anti-Climacus; and, with another volume by Johannes Climacus—over twice the size of its predecessor— *Concluding Unscientific Postscript to the Philosophical Fragments* (1846), thought by Kierkegaard to be his last left-handed work!

From his right hand, under his own name, and during the same period, he also wrote and paid for the publication of lengthy essays, volumes of them, intended to be complementary to the left hand literature—essays that he meant to be uplifting and upbuilding or, as we know eighteen of them, *Edifying Discourses*. To these he added many other discourses or collections with titles such as *Works of Love* and the pair, *For Self-Examination* and *Judge for Yourself!* In all, Kierkegaard's writings—papers and journals, even a book by Climacus that Søren Kierkegaard chose not to publish, *De Omnibus Dubitandum Est*—form a collection that would overburden the average bookshelf.

To contemporaries, his plan to offer twin but purposefully contrary authorships went virtually unnoticed, a successful strategy. Still, Kierkegaard was discouraged to learn that his readers were much more enthused about his left hand works than about the writings to which he affixed his own name, and the latter drew unwanted criticism late in his life.

Except for *The Concept of Irony*, the university dissertation that would normally go into the library, Kierkegaard's first publication was *Either/Or*, often the work with which readers new to Kierkegaard begin—and, unfortunately, a work whose views they may attribute to him personally rather than to the characters he describes. Søren Kierkegaard often takes credit for the publication of the pseudonymous or left hand works; indeed, toward the end of his life he took full responsibility for everything he published. However, his intention always was to allow each work to stand by itself, to represent life's collisions of views and values by authors and characters that speak for themselves. The reader can decide how true to the human condition they are.

Either/Or is somewhat forbidding, a two-volume work divided by the title, in which opposing views of life are presented as a major choice. Through the pseudonymous editor, Victor Eremita—who maintains the left-handed character by explaining that their chance discovery and interest prompted him to publish them—the volumes introduce the reader to three of the major "stages," dimensions or modes of life that ground these writings: esthetic, ethical, and to a lesser degree, religious.

The esthetic life dominates *Either*, the first volume, with diverse writings that include a diary attributed to a certain "seducer" and even a sermon whose authorship is unknown. Mostly, however, the pieces center on the reflections of an unnamed "young man," an esthete through and through. That is, it is an outlook that perhaps we have by nature, governed by reference to pleasure and pain, emotional disposition, self-interest, immediacy, the interesting, and the dull. It is essentially a mode we encounter that is indifferent—if not opposed—to the ethical and the religious. One might suppose that at its lowest levels the esthetic also includes, though only implied, the agnostic who claims no certainty of the supernatural, the atheist who dismisses any belief in it at all, and perhaps the criminal mind that can be aggressively disposed to skirt the ethical and the lawful.

To the "young man," boredom is the fundamental evil. In philosophical terms the outlook approaches ancient Hedonism, just short of the utilitarian views of English thinkers and writers born earlier than Kierkegaard, like Jeremy Bentham (1748-1832) and John Stuart Mill (1806-1873). To them, whatever results in pleasure is good and, for most of them, ethical; and whatever leads to pain is bad and should be avoided.

The second volume, *Or*, presents in two lengthy letters to the young esthete the rigorously ethical point of view taken by a judge, William, who seems to know the young man, understands his chosen way of life, and offers some no-nonsense fatherly-like counsel to him. Judge William reflects a view of ethics that generally approaches that of the great eighteenth century German philosopher, Immanuel Kant (1724-1804), a view governed by the duties and responsibilities we develop around marriage, family, citizenship, and the virtues of honesty and justice. To Kant, the good life, the moral life, is not governed by momentary pain and pleasure, but by a universal imperative, like a law of nature, which holds that one must always intend to act in a way that is acceptable to good reason, though not absurdly, but universally applicable to every person in every time and place. To the Judge, it is the right thing, the most satisfying thing to do. But it is a fundamental choice, a logical disjunction: esthetic or ethical, either/or. No compromise is possible among such competing values.

The young man thinks otherwise. Cynicism is best, life is more "both/and" than "either/or." At bottom, choice does not matter, nothing really matters; indeed, he virtually subscribes to nihilism, the prospect that nothing is real or worthwhile, except perhaps what is new, interesting, fashionable, culturally acceptable, exciting at the moment, strictly transient, relative and not absolute. He seems to lack consistency, proportion, long-term perspective. In a poetic introduction to a discourse on the improbable idea of any either/or, the young man notes:

> My life is meaningless How dreadful boredom is—how dreadfully boring. If I were offered all the glories of the world or all the torments of the world, one would move me no more than the other; I would not turn over to the other side either to attain or to avoid. I am dying death. And what could divert me? Well, if I managed to see a faithfulness that withstood every ordeal [Danish, *Provelse*], an enthusiasm that endured everything, a faith that moved mountains; if I were to become aware of an idea that joined the finite and the infinite. But my soul's poisonous doubt consumes everything (*Ibid.*, p. 43).

(Note: These fundamental themes are seen in Kierkegaard's further writings.)

In fact the young man wrote a brief discourse entitled "Either/Or," which may have suggested to Eremita, the editor, the title of *Either/Or*. It opens with the thought that whatever you do, you will regret:

> Marry, and you will regret it. Do not marry, and you will also regret it. Marry or do not marry, you will regret it either way. Laugh at the stupidities of the world, and you will regret it; weep over them, and you will also regret it. Hang yourself, and you will regret it. Do not hang yourself, and you will also regret it. This, gentlemen, is the quintessence of all the wisdom of life (*Ibid.*, p.44).

Either way, it makes no difference; neither is meaningful for his existence.

In the second volume the Judge tells the young man that, though he may not recognize it, his true condition is one of "despair"—a major topic covered at greater length later. The Judge warns him that the inevitable upshot of living and believing as he does is no answer and does nothing to relieve his situation. A better way is to live by something like the Golden Rule which requires personal discipline and is not always pleasant; one's duty should be governed by principles that are higher than individual whim or impulse. There is a more effective way to give greater meaning to one's life than merely to seek the pleasurable and avoid the painful. It is by willing to choose:

> The choice itself is crucial for the content of the personality: through the choice the personality submerges itself in that which is being chosen, and when it does not choose, it withers away in atrophy. Your choice is an esthetic choice, but an esthetic choice is no choice. On the whole, to choose is an intrinsic and stringent term for the ethical. The only absolute Either/Or is the choice between good and evil, but this is also absolutely ethical. What, then, is

it that I separate in my Either/Or? Is it good and evil? No, I only want to bring you to the point where this choice truly has meaning for you. It is on this that everything turns (*Ibid.*, p.72f.).

At this point the Judge subtly encourages the young man to look inward, to examine his personal self, to recognize his despair for what it is, and to come to terms with what he confessed earlier was "my soul's poisonous doubt." He is leading a poetic existence which, though it has left him desperately unhappy, is not a matter of destiny. Ironically, the Judge avers, only by recognizing that the esthetic life without decisiveness leads to indifference and despair can the solution to his condition emerge—and the solution is to despair, and despair decisively! For that is the nature of the human predicament:

> Choose despair, then, because despair itself is a choice, because one can doubt [*tvivle*] without choosing it, but one cannot despair [*fortvivle*] without choosing it. And in despairing a person chooses again, and what then does he choose? He chooses himself, not in his immediacy, not as this accidental individual, but he chooses himself in his eternal validity (*Ibid.*, p.77f).

Here the Judge only hints at a view of the self and its "eternal validity," one that Søren Kierkegaard develops in later works; and, because it is central to them, the idea of despair as a fundamental aspect of the human condition deserves its own treatment later on.

For now, however, it may be enough to note the Judge's reference to "doubt." Current thinking, he says, has popularly adopted the position made famous by Rene Descartes (1596-1650), the great seventeenth century French mathematician and philosopher who attempted to show that the very act of doubting, a rational act, alone can logically prove what is real and what is not: I doubt, I think, therefore I am. Reality is the product of strictly rational deduction. However, Judge William puts it another way:

> Doubt is thought's despair; despair is personality's doubt. That is why I cling so firmly to the defining characteristic "to choose;" it is my watchword, the nerve in my life-view, and that I do have, even if I can in no way presume to have [an all-encompassing theory]. Doubt is the inner movement in thought itself, and in my doubt I conduct myself as impersonally as possible (*Ibid.*, p. 77f).

Again, the Judge urges the young man to embrace the self he has, as he puts it:

> But what is this self of mine? If I were to speak of a first moment, a first expression for it, then my answer is this: It is the most abstract of all, and yet in itself it is also the most concrete of all—it is freedom (*Ibid.*, p. 80).

That is to say, choose despair! For

> despair's choice is "myself." A human being's eternal dignity lies in this, that he can gain a history. The divine in him lies in this, that he himself, if he so chooses, can give this history continuity, because it gains that, not when it is a summary of what has taken place or has happened to me, but only when it is my personal deed in such a way that even that which has happened to me is transformed and transferred from necessity to freedom (*Ibid.*, p. 80).

In short, while one must accept one's heritage and personal identity, one also has the freedom to change one's way of life. And that is possible by virtue of the self's nature, its freedom, an eternally valid resource.

But now we should consider more closely Kierkegaard's concept of "stages," particularly as he embodies them esthetically in a cast of characters described in Hilarius Bookbinder's *Stages on Life's Way*.

STAGES

In his own way in *Either/Or,* Judge William introduces the inner structure of the principal stages or modes with which Kierkegaard characterizes human existence. The esthetic and ethical modes are clearly in different spheres. But he also alludes to a third, the religious. In fact he might have, but did not, introduce certain "boundary" stages or dimensions of existence as well, such as "irony" and "humor" which, as we will see, are also of some importance to Kierkegaard. And yet, the Judge notes, if the "young man" fails to appreciate that the esthetical, ethical, and religious ways of life are really complementary as well as diverse—a complex unity of these various spheres—his life will have little or no meaning. Life contains all such structures in varying degrees, even within the esthetic dimension. What governs one's existence is a matter of personal passion.

In short, each domain has its own rationale, its own spirit, and no argument or compelling case for one is sufficient to persuade a person simply to abandon the sphere in which he exists for the sake of another. You are what you passionately choose. Yet, the conflict of values between one domain and another is so sharp that, as Kierkegaard notes in great detail later, it represents a "paradox," an intellectual obstacle to rationality (and Descartes) that is overcome only by taking a "leap of faith." Though absurd to reason, it is a movement that has the effect not of completely divorcing one domain or set of values for another, but of dethroning or subordinating or transcending one's former commitments in order to assume a more desirable perspective, with a more passionate commitment at stake. That is, a person becomes ethical by a resolute act of will; and an ethical person becomes religious by an act of faith. Both acts are forms of passion, not logical deduction, in steps of ever greater intensity. Willing to choose is the means to be ethical.

The work entitled *Stages on Life's Way*, by the pseudonymous publisher Hilarius Bookbinder, includes among various essays a section entitled "*In Vino Veritas*," a recollection related by William Afham, a contributing author. Afham makes a point of introducing it by distinguishing a writer's remembrance from his "recollection," the latter a capacity to give meaning and personal character to the memory. (Keep this concept in mind.) The subsequent recollection mainly depicts the esthetic domain now based on the views of a new cast of characters—except for a familiar one, the "young man."

Apparently, however, Kierkegaard hoped to dramatize just how distant the esthete is in varying degrees from the ethical and the religious. The Afham piece describes a banquet scene reminiscent of Plato's famous dialogue, *The Symposium*, where each person present is obliged to say what he thinks of love—but only after each is well on the road to intoxication. A review of Plato's work, a somewhat loftier dialogue than Afham's, is worth a comparison.

Typically, by making each participant express his views of the nature of love, Plato intends eventually to characterize "ideal love," a conversation he reserves for Diotima, a seer, as reported by Socrates and introduced by other guests—though the real Socrates would likely have examined each speaker more thoroughly in his accustomed fashion and would not necessarily have embraced Plato's belief. Plato is looking for, though he is not a participant, a concept of love that is superior, essential to, but also common to all opinions and kinds of love—a love that can be succinctly and rationally defined and by which every other notion or experience is an imperfect reflection of the real thing. The real thing is virtually something heavenly, divine. Socrates begins the affair, a first stage of the argument, by asserting that love must be desire of something, and since we cannot truly be said to desire what we already have, it must be a desire for something that we lack. Agathon, a fellow participant, is content simply to praise love as a thing of beauty, but Socrates responds that we also love excellence in all its forms, so both cannot be essential to love, though love may aspire to have them. This view he attributes to what he learned from the seer, Diotima, who adds that love is neither good nor bad, which are extremes; rather, it is something somewhere between them. Socrates asks her if perhaps love is therefore some divine spirit that benevolently invades human life; but Diotima rules that idea out, because the gods alone possess goodness and that is not the sole nature of love. So what is love, Socrates asks. Diotima states that it is a mean between the extremes of human and divine, between ignorance and wisdom; love seeks the latter, but from its beginnings in human ignorance and curiosity. (For Plato, this kind of seeking might well have identified Socrates.)

A second stage for the discussion is set by the question: If we desire the good and the happiness that results from it—which all desire—why is it that all are not always in love? The answer is that there are at least two kinds of love: one is sexual or erotic love, the upshot of which is procreation by the body; another is the love that creative people—philosophers (meaning "lovers of wisdom"), poets, and artists have for their work, which is the expression of mind or soul (in a secular sense). Love's object is experienced in the children we sire and in the works we create, a bifurcation of the self (body and soul) that desires a kind of immortality—a likely Greek counterpart for Judge Williams' reference to one's "eternal validity," one's link to the supernatural.

In a final stage of the speeches, Plato begins to get his wish: Diotima is said to explain that by loving a particular object of beauty, one begins to perceive in it what is common to all beautiful objects; one then understands that the beauty seen by the soul (the capacity for reflection) is more excellent than that of the body (perception by the senses), and soon one is able to survey abstractly, independently of the senses, the entire realm of beauty. With a final effort of the intellect, one will comprehend what is universal about it, what is truly common to all instances of love, its "essence," the eternal, Ideal Beauty—and love, particularly the love of wisdom, or philosophy, is the best guide to reach this ultimate insight. With wisdom, one always loves the ideal.

Matters at the banquet become a little less sophisticated after that. Alcibiades, an outlandish admirer of Socrates, enters drunk. But he speaks the truth by noting, as everyone knows, that while Socrates may not be outwardly handsome (in fact he was reputed to be ugly), he is nonetheless inwardly noble, whether, as it was well attested in Athens, Socrates examined the views of fellow citizens or when he fought in battle—and he is also quite able to drink anyone under the table, with no lapse in mental penetration!

The dialogue ends with everyone either asleep or drunk except Socrates, Agathon, and the famous comedy writer, Aristophanes (450-385 B.C.), who in one of his dramas portrayed Socrates reclining blissfully on a cloud. Ironically, Socrates ends the banquet by wondering if the genius of comedy is essentially the same as that of tragedy!

In Hilarius Bookbinder's *Stages*, there is the essay by Afham entitled "*In Vino Veritas*"—in wine there is truth—which also describes a banquet scene where each guest is expected to make a speech, but about erotic love. The banquet was first proposed by a group of friends over coffee (a situation based, perhaps, on occasions Kierkegaard and his friends from the university frequently had together). According to Bookbinder, one of the group known as "The Seducer" proposed that the banquet be held immediately, spur of the moment, intentionally leaving little or no time to prepare. Moreover, the surroundings should be new to all, and afterwards all evidence of the affair should be destroyed. The Seducer's requirements of course suggest the character of the immediate, the new and the transient identified with the esthetic outlook in *Either/Or*.

In fact one of the banquet's planners is the latter's publisher, Victor Eremita. He reveals his own esthetic outlook as he proposes that the affair should not even be discussed in advance, and that to be successful it should be spontaneous because spontaneity is the most divine of categories. He also sets some outrageous conditions: The affair should be the most splendid occasion imaginable, or at least possible, which is more seductive than the actual; the meal should be fit for a gourmet and graced with more wine than it seems possible to exhaust; the place should be heavily scented with the finest perfumes; and it must by all means have a splashing fountain in ceaseless motion.

Without Constantine Constantius, one of the group, an experimental psychologist (and the subsequent author of *Repetition*, as we shall see), the proposals might never have taken shape. Still, shortly after the meeting, he sent invitations to the group for a banquet to be held that very evening, an occasion labeled with the theme *"In Vino Veritas"* with the instruction that no speech could be offered except under the influence, *"in vino."* Remarkably, as the guests arrived they found a setting very much as Eremita wanted; and after a few courses of the meal Constantine asked that the speeches begin (provided they were fueled by sufficient wine) and that the topic should be love.

The "young man" (from *Either*) opens by confessing that he has no great experience with love, but that to him the sheer thought of love is most intriguing, more so than any desire one might have to seduce or fall for or court a woman by allowing emotion to rule over dispassionate thought. Besides, the goal of love is marriage and family, and the young man dreads such responsibilities. To his cynical way of thinking, love is some mysterious power that makes a man like a puppet moved by strings that some other person, a woman, pulls. He says:

> I will not love anybody before I have fathomed the thought of love, and that I am not able to do; on the contrary, I have reached the conclusion that love is comic. So I am unwilling to love; but by this precaution the danger has not been avoided, for since I do not know what the lovable is, how it attacks me, or how it attacks a woman with reference to me, I cannot be sure of knowing whether I have avoided the danger. This is tragic, in a sense that there is something which exercises its power everywhere and yet cannot be grasped by thought (Reidar Thomte, *Kierkegaard's Philosophy of Religion*, Princeton University Press, 1948, p. 18f.).

Constantine speaks next. To take women seriously is a joke, as the young man suggests, not in an esthetic sense but rather in an ethical sense. At best, women are ethically imperfect and can never be taken seriously, contrary to men who by nature express themselves absolutely, forthrightly. To suggest they have an ideality is illusory; we pump them up into something they are not when instead we should pump the air out of them. "Just as one man finds his amusement in balancing a cane upon his nose, so and not otherwise has the lover in commerce with his lady the most incomparable amusement." Even Plato, notes the author, finds her an incomplete human ideal (*Ibid.*, p. 19f.).

Eremita tends to agree, but is confused. The romantic life forced upon a woman works to make her existence meaningless: occasionally it has significance, but just as often none; one day she strikes you as the epitome of attractiveness, the next day just another woman. True, she can be of great importance to a man by inspiring him, say, to become a great writer—but only at the right historical moment, after which she is of little consequence and might as well become unfaithful to him.

> A love affair is a relatively simple thing—but not a marriage! It seems impossible to determine whether it is something pagan or Christian, something pious or something secular, something civic or a little of everything or a duty, a partnership, an expedience, the thing to do! (*Ibid.*, p. 20f.).

The Fashion Designer, a women's tailor, follows this with an oration that focuses on what he knows clearly from experience about a woman's nature: the fashionable. She is basically vain, a prisoner of the mirror where she sees herself in the endless array of garments, shoes, hair styles, and "that phantom which is formed by the unnatural intercourse of feminine reflection with feminine reflection, i.e., fashion" (*Ibid.*, p. 21).

Finally, the guest referred to as Johannes the Seducer (from *Either/Or*?) speaks about women in terms that unashamedly reflect his nickname. Seductive and delicate, women were made by the gods to be enjoyed, and that is all there is to it. There is no universal or ideal woman (contrary to Plato); every woman is different, each a unique object of a man's momentary emotion and passion. "The gods made her perfect, but then they hid all this from her in the ignorance of innocence and modesty. [T]here is no allurement so absolute as that of innocence, and no temptation so fascinating as that of modesty, and no deception so incomparable as woman" (*Ibid.*, p. 22).

The banquet ends with each guest smashing his wine glass against the wall in a show of esthetic bravado. From their nature none of the guests can be said to be unaware of the demands of the ethical. They are simply disinterested in what one morally ought to think or to do.

At the point when Kierkegaard revealed his responsibility for the entire authorship, pseudonyms and all, he interpreted their personalities in this way: There is still a chance for the young man to choose to be ethical, and Kierkegaard depicts him as "melancholy thought;" Constantine is perhaps too dispassionate and insensitive due to a career as an experimental psychologist and occasional consultant, and so he reveals less about himself than he might; Eremita is in a state Kierkegaard calls "sympathetic irony" for his view that, while tragic, a woman's fate is servitude to man; the Fashion Designer is simply demonic, cynical in his reduction of women to whatever is fashionable; and the Seducer, obsessed with immediacy and newness, is the best example of the esthete.

As Thomte finds in Kierkegaard's notes, the moment these personalities open their mouths, the reader can hear in their words the perdition and the condemnation corresponding to their attitudes. Following the motto of *"In Vino Veritas,"* Kierkegaard borrowed a line from the poet Lichtenberg: "Such works are mirrors; when a monkey peers into them, no apostle can look out"—which suggests that as readers pass judgment on such testimony, they reveal their own inner personality, their own governing attitude (*Ibid.*, p. 23). For Kierkegaard, it is also a form of the indirect communication that is intentionally characteristic of his writings.

Similar attitudinal collisions and stage-like themes are picked up in subsequent works—for example, Constantine's own little book, *Repetition*. As you recall from the banquet, his perspective is rather clinical and objective as you would expect a student of behavior to be. It is hard to tell just where he falls between the esthetic and the ethical, and he seems to be struggling over the question, particularly as a result of recent experiences with patients.

One of his patients is—again, the "young man"—whose troubled mind surrounding his breach of engagement (sound familiar?) suggested a clash of esthetic and ethical values. According to Constantine, the young man revealed that he could not marry and still be true to his own nature; marriage would mean that he must change, and things would never be quite the same again. He had discovered this disturbing notion of change also after his holidays in Berlin, where he had two quite different experiences. On the first trip there he had a wonderful, memorable time; he especially enjoyed the opera as well as the lively places he visited, so much so that he looked forward to a second holiday there. However, on the second trip his earlier pleasures could not be repeated: The opera was poor, the food and lodging were not what he had known, and the change was most disappointing. It struck him that a repetition of that sort is not possible, and he was depressed. So how, Constantine wondered, should he counsel the young man?

Before he could resolve his question he came across the story of Job in the Old Testament. As the story goes, God unexpectedly visited Job with one miserable affliction after the other, for reasons Job could not understand. On the contrary, Job knew he had been a good man, upright and righteous in his prosperity before God. Why, Job asked again and again, would God crush him so, taking everything including his children away from him, leaving him with a suffering next to death, and worse—no answer even from God? In the face of his critics, his so-called comforters who insisted he must have sinned against God and now should repent, Job was adamant about his innocence. One day, Job believed, God would explain his terrible sufferings—a situation absurd to himself and to others, but for different reasons—perhaps a "paradox" contrary to reason. Still, Job insists, "though He slay me, yet will I trust Him" (Job 13, King James Version).

As it happens, God does answer Job "out of the whirlwind," scolding him for being faithless and charging him to be God's most righteous servant, after which God restored twofold all that Job lost, except his children. In short, Job experienced a repetition or reduplication of his life.

Constantine decided to pass the story along to the young man who subsequently came to the realization that perhaps he too might experience a repetition, like Job. However, it was not what he expected. What he got instead was the news that his ex-fiance had married another man. Still, he was not crushed by the news, but in fact he himself was changed; his personality was reintegrated by this strange kind of repetition. Emotionally he felt like a new person—an allusion by Kierkegaard, perhaps, to St. Paul's characterization of religious conversion through godly redemption, and a hint of a new stage. In any case the young man experienced a transformation:

> I am myself again. This "self" that someone else would not pick up off the street I have once again. The split that was in my being is healed; I am unified again. The anxieties of sympathy that were sustained and nourished by my pride are no longer there to disintegrate and disrupt. Is there not, then, a repetition? Did I not get everything double? Did I not get myself again and precisely in such a way that I might have a double sense of its meaning? Compared with such a repetition, what is a repetition of worldly possessions, which is indifferent toward the qualification of the spirit? Only his children did Job not receive double again, for a human life cannot be redoubled that way. Here only repetition of the spirit is possible, even though it is never so perfect in time as in eternity, which is the true repetition (*TEK*, op. cit., p.114)

Do you suppose the young man ever made the "leap" to the ethical? Or to the religious? The possibilities are there, but we will never know.

Thus, Kierkegaard allows all of his characters and authors to allude, if at times obliquely or indirectly, to the significant domains or stages—and their passions, attitudes, values, uncertainties, and possibilities—occupying the human condition. He also introduces new aspects of the self, such as reduplication and spirit, as we shall see. Mainly, however, Johannes the Seducer in *Stages* is regarded by Kierkegaard as the ultimate esthete. However, there is little question but that Judge William would have consigned all of the banquet's guests, not just the young man (but with the possible exception of Constantine) to the realm of human despair, and that is a topic we must explore at some length next.

DESPAIR

With the virtually unique preoccupations of his authorship, Kierkegaard gave birth to a movement we today call Existentialism. Thinkers and writers, notably the French intellectuals Jean-Paul Sartre (1905-1980) and Albert Camus (1913-1960) in our time, assumed the view and were certainly influenced by Kierkegaard. What is this all about?

In the early history of thought prior to the Greeks, to whom we credit the beginnings of Western Civilization, there is a tempting resemblance to the Existentialist movement in what we have popularly come to call "philosophy of life." For example, Oriental philosophers such as Confucius (551-479 B.C.) in the *I Ching*, or Lao-tse (604-531 B.C.) and his theory of the *Tao de Ching*, wrote or influenced major views that once instructed leaders and common folk alike on how to cope with and capitalize on the exigencies of daily human affairs. Indeed, these writings continue to be studied to this day. However, with a different focus on reality, the Egyptians (with whom well-known Grecian thinkers often went to study) were somewhat more externally oriented. Their engineers and theorists applied their knowledge of astronomy and mathematics—they discovered *pi* and other geometrical functions known to the third century B.C. Greek mathematician Euclid—to the building of the pyramids and other massive monuments.

Both before and during the centuries following Socrates, most of the great scientists, philosophers, and theologians from Aristotle (384-322 B.C.), Plato's successor, to Isaac Newton (1624-1727), until after Descartes, preoccupied themselves with realities commonly thought to be external to and ultimately responsible for the perceptual world. That world of course embraces all the "objects" we experience, that is, the people, cars, homes, jobs, computers, cell phones, *et al*, much of which is born of the technology we enjoy. These thinkers theorized with abstract explanatory concepts such as space, time, motion, matter, causality, and other presumed dimensions, forces, and laws of nature to which the human and animal kingdoms are subject. And, they devised impressive hypotheses and even whole systems, like Albert Einstein's general theory of relativity, to explain the world as we know it. Like Plato, they sought the universal or absolute reality, the ultimate crux and origin of things, in short, the "essence" or rational, otherworldly ideal that explains and lies behind all "objective," empirical knowledge.

Even Socrates early in life did his share of speculation about the cosmos; for example, he considered, as his predecessors had, whether all there is could be reduced to a single element such as earth, air, fire, water, even particles like atoms. But it was not satisfying for him. He subsequently decided there was first a more important task, namely, to understand the self, a reality about which he felt we are certainly as ignorant and he, ironically, most of all—although a famous Athenian seer (not Diotima) at the local temple declared that he was by his own confession the wisest of all! From the *Dialogues of Plato* we know that he determined to suspend his early interest in possible cosmic realities in favor of self-knowledge and the careful use of human reason for examining the ideas we carelessly tend to cherish.

Kierkegaard picked up the Socratic torch. He joined with a few other thinkers he admired, such as the German mystic and critic of Kant, Johann Georg Hamann (1730-1788), whose little book, *Socratic Memorabilia*, significantly influenced Kierkegaard and may have prompted him to write his own later book, *Philosophical Fragments*. Like Socrates, he too turned to the self, to personal existence with all its uncertain potential for good and evil, in order to lay bare the fundamental layers of experience we have as human beings: anxiety, doubt, loss, dread, terror, despair, and many other intimations of the self's nature which daunt and disrupt existence. And it is on this range of all-too-human, "existential" experience—contrary to Platonic "essence"—that Existentialists like Sartre, who learned from the terrors of the Nazi occupation in World War II, and Camus, who wrote brilliantly of human plague and suicide before his own tragic death, are focused.

Among the great thinkers of whom Kierkegaard was especially critical was G. W. F. Hegel (1770-1831), a German philosopher following Kant, who wrote several popular and extensive treatises that proposed to explain everything in terms of a dynamic world view, a universally embracing triangle of cosmic change. Hegel's systematic and voluminous work can in no sense be justly described here, but perhaps an example will help.

Let's say that a particular historical period is first opposed (but not wholly eliminated) by a second period contrary to it, then blended or synthesized in company with it (preserving the best of both periods) to create a third period—that in turn becomes a new period to be opposed, synthesized, etc. On a cosmic scale this is basically the nature of all change; however, in other ways as well, there is virtually no area of reality Hegel did not theorize about—including, as we noted earlier, "irony." While Kierkegaard studied Hegel and occasionally adopted his categories for his own purposes, he had no time for such global theories or "systems"—castles, he suggested, in which no one actually exists.

As we know, Kierkegaard's pseudonymous publishers and characters represent particular modes of life, embodied self-understandings of human existence—as we experience it. The task is to understand what our serious, self-conscious reflection—inwardness—tells us. Kant, for example, spoke of the dual nature of the self that accounts for the conscious dialogue we have with ourselves, even argument, that includes the personal challenges of conscience in the deliberations of ethical matters, right and wrong. Comparably, Kierkegaard's dialectical style demands that the reader reflect the many possible, often opposing reflections of self-examination—as if we were carrying on a dialogue with Socrates and always at the risk of missing something important, or worse, of self-contradiction.

As we examine Kierkegaard's view of the self in greater part later, it will be helpful also to understand the principle he adopted for this purpose: *unum noris omnes* (if you know one, you know all). That is, if you reveal your own nature, you also understand the nature of others. Only Kierkegaard's readers can confirm or deny this principle; only they can say, "I know what he means; I've experienced it." It turns out that several of Kierkegaard's later works are subtitled to suggest they are "psychic" studies, for example, examinations of anxiety, doubt, and of course, despair. In reflection, the self is finally revealed to be more than the conventionally-accepted duality of mind and body; it is also spirit, a component that can transcend the other two with its eternal character. But we will say more of this later.

What is self-conscious reflection likely to tell us about ourselves and about the human condition? To Kierkegaard, the most pervasive sense is despair, along with a related sense, anxiety. Despair, as we commonly experience it, takes many forms: despair at not being successful, at not being noticed, at not knowing what the future holds, at wondering what death is like and when it will come, at having no close friend or understanding parent, at the loss of someone dear, at old age, and so forth. Basically, as Judge William says about the young man in *Either/Or*, his despair is in not being willing to accept himself for the cynical, troubled self he has; in short, he is not willing to be himself, to face up to who and what he is, coupled with his conviction that there is nothing he can do about it. The young man acknowledges the ideals to which people aspire, like vigorous health, great beauty, striking personality, wealth, talent, a sense of well being. But he concludes they are not within his grasp, his control, and so he retreats from those aspirations into a life of immediate pleasures—without any commitments, if he can help it. Destiny, he feels, has played a trick on him, and that is the way it is. It no doubt strikes him as ludicrous to be told by the Judge that by accepting himself, he must accept his despair! Still, that is exactly what the Judge means: Accept the despair, assume it for what it is, and with all your willpower, be decisive about it. Summon all your mental strength and choose! What possible sense can that make to the young man?

Recall also the Judge's talk of doubt. As a student at the university, Kierkegaard wrote a book-length treatise which he never published entitled *De Omnibus Dubitandum Est* (1842-1843), (everything is doubtful, or doubtable). *De Omnibus*, whose pseudonymous author is Johannes Climacus, is a response to one of Descartes' famous discourses in which the philosopher, musing in his study, notes that everything he perceives or thinks about seems to have no more substance, no more reality than a dream. Everything is doubtful, until he finally realizes that his very doubt cannot be doubted—that his doubt is an expression of thought, and that he has therefore rationally deduced at least the reality of himself: *cogito, ergo sum* (I think, therefore I am)—a favorite T-shirt saying even today. To deny this conclusion is to commit a logical contradiction. It is the principle of rationality that alone has relieved his doubt, and with that he continues to deduce objective reality—including the existence of God! Descartes becomes identified in subsequent history as the Father of Rationalism.

In his response, Climacus acknowledges the allurement of this principle of rationality but develops at length his own doubts concerning its primacy for existence. Though doubt is a very real condition of it, and reason is fundamental to understanding, there is much more to reflection and inwardness. As Kierkegaard puts it in the words of the Judge to the young man, doubt is indeed the despair of the intellect, but despair is the doubt that troubles the self and pervades one's existence. Despair is of greater consequence and, above all, is the young man's problem.

In subsequent writings such as *The Concept of Anxiety* by Vigilius Haufniensis, despair is described as "unawakened anxiety," latent in human "ignorance" (borrowed from Socrates), the doubt that troubles existence. It is an unfulfilled state of primal innocence, with a notable unawareness of that third component, soul or "spirit."

With another nod to Socrates, Vigilius goes on to note that in the initial state of innocence, apparently prior to conscious reflection, a person is ignorant of their natural condition and is not yet qualified by spirit, which alone is the mark of an "authentic self." Socrates was authentic, Vigilius says in his opening motto, because he distinguished between what he understood and what he did not understand—an expression taken from Hamann's *Socratic Memorabilia*. As if to allude to Descartes' musing, Vigilius states that though the spirit has not yet imprinted the self, it is not absent, it is only "dreaming" in a person's ignorant, thoughtless condition.

Actually, he claims the spirit is at peace, with no strife or concern, because there is nothing to strive for or against. It is a state of nothingness or nihilism—which once awakened leads inevitably in one's first act of choice to the sense of "anxiety." The dreaming, potentially but not yet anxious self therefore knows no fear. It is, by its latent nature, free, but only, in Vigilius' language, as "possibility." The state, he suggests, approaches "melancholy"—another condition shared by Hamann and Søren Kierkegaard (and note the "young man" in *The Stages*). It is a condition prior to the awakening of freedom and the possibility of developing spirit—a level or dimension of the self other than, and in addition to, the familiar notion of the human self's duality of mind and body.

This is the stuff of existence and Existentialism, the human condition, the self: dreaming, innocence, ignorance, nothingness, despair, fear, anxiety, melancholy, suffering, guilt, alienation, freedom, spirit, authenticity. Though the Socratic quest for self-knowledge may not be a so-called "hard science" such as physics or mathematics, it is a daily, lifelong task of equally profound significance, and few if any writers in intellectual history have tracked the nature of existence, as we experience it, as Kierkegaard.

Judge William's analysis is a fairly unsophisticated version of despair, though no less penetrating to the truth of the young man's condition. He clearly has his finger on the pulse of the young man's rather meaningless life, of course, but presumably he is unaware of Vigilius' studied analysis other than to prescribe added decisiveness to the young man's freedom—along with more despair—as a prelude to the possibility of becoming ethical. Nonetheless, Vigilius' reading of the self is applicable also to the young man, though preoccupation with esthetic immediacy, pleasure and pain, and the futility of choice, have given way to a despair that his capacity for freedom, his ethical possibility, cannot abide. Still, there is hope for the young man. With Job in *Repetition*, he did experience a reduplication, right?

There is much more to the self as we shall see in what follows; however, the predominance of despair, a condition well beyond Kierkegaard's dramatic expression for his painful separation from Regine, is amply evident throughout much of his authorship.

SELF

We have considered the esthetic nature of the self. Its ethical and religious demands are decidedly more rigorous. For Judge William, to do the right thing, the ethical thing, is not the pleasure that may or may not result as the fortunate outcome of one's efforts. On the contrary and independently of the result, good or bad, in Immanuel Kant's view it is the good "intention" of the will that counts. One's free will must correspond to the imperative to do what is right for everyone at all times, if at all possible, and not just, as John Stuart Mill held, for most people most of the time. If, according to Mill's philosophical nemesis, Kant, there is such a thing as a moral order in reality, it requires nothing less than a universally acknowledged ethical imperative comparable to a law of nature.

However, for Kierkegaard the ethical self is also flawed. One's good intentions may mean everything, but as the saying goes, the road to hell is paved with them. It also calls to mind the New Testament caveat cited by the Apostle Paul: The good that I would, I cannot; and the good that I can, I will not. With a subtle nod to the religious self as well, Kierkegaard initially represents the predicament facing the ethical self in a work entitled *Fear and Trembling* by the pseudonymous author Johannes de Silentio, the silent one. It is based on the Old Testament story of Abraham and Isaac and is certainly a "must" for first-time readers of Kierkegaard. (Is it also a subtle reflection of his father's guilty need for atonement?)

Like Johannes Climacus, the university student of Descartes, de Silentio prefaces the account of God's requirement of Abraham that he sacrifice Isaac with a fairly academic treatment of tragedy and heroism as it is played out in history and literature. In fact he first pays homage also to Descartes for his honest approach to the principle of doubt—believing, however, that it had the unfortunate effect among his followers of leaving no room for "faith." De Silentio denies that he is a philosopher; he is merely an admirer of Abraham, whom he regards as the Father of Faith.

The story is developed dramatically as it reflects what Abraham, Isaac, and Sarah each must have thought as they puzzled over God's command. Nonetheless, while he struggled with the collisions of despair and doubt, Abraham obeyed. He took his young son, the one given miraculously to Sarah in her old age, up to Mount Moriah. He bound Isaac to the sacrificial pedestal and drew his knife with demonic terror as he prepared to kill him. Absurdly, he could do this horrific thing only by believing that somehow God would once again restore all to him (like Job, an act of repetition or reduplication).

Then, as the story goes, God spared Isaac's life at the last moment. Unlike figures of the past, Abraham did not have to become a tragic hero; he is instead a "knight of faith" who became so by believing—absurdly, despite what Kant's imperative cannot abide—that God would somehow make it up to him and to Sarah. This he believes even if he has to commit what all, especially those committed to what God had earlier commanded, would surely regard as murder. It is "the leap of faith."

The absurdities are enormous: God the Holy One's command, unthinkably contrary to God's own early promise and gift of Isaac to Sarah; Abraham's belief that all would somehow be restored after the sacrifice; prescribed murder, contrary to the commandments—and Kant's universally acknowledged moral order. None of this is comprehensible from a rational, logical point of view. It is a "paradox" that utterly stymies the mind and cripples the ethical self by setting it aside, suspending it—de Silentio describes it as a "teleological [purposeful] suspension of the ethical"—for the sake of a good that is higher, greater. From an objective, dispassionate point of view, de Silentio concludes that the act of faith commits one so clearly and strictly to a relationship with God that ethical relationships to family, community, and country may at times have to be set aside. In short, there are situations, dilemmas, predicaments in life that the ethical self cannot resolve. This new dimension, faith, cannot be overlooked.

Clearly, there is a fatal flaw in Judge William's plea to the young man to become ethical, except perhaps for the sense of despair that cannot have escaped Abraham and Sarah as they anguished over the thought of losing Isaac. The Judge identifies two forms of despair: not willing to be oneself, the esthetic self; and/or willing to be oneself, the ethical self. In Vigilius Haufniensis' treatment of *The Concept of Anxiety*, the self is said also to experience anxiety, which, we noted, is latent in the self's ignorance and undistinguished innocence. Anxiety is brought to life by some first act of choice, of free will—the same freedom, presumably, that is fundamental for becoming an ethical self.

As Anti-Climacus explains in *The Sickness Unto Death*, however, this is prelude to the emergence of "spirit" which, also latent but dreaming, finally reveals the "authentic self." In a summary heading to his treatise he identifies despair as "the sickness unto death," a sickness of the spirit, of the self. In a challenging though not impossible statement, Anti-Climacus writes:

> A human being is spirit. But what is spirit? Spirit is the self. But what is the self? The self is a relation that relates itself to itself or is the relation's relating itself to itself in the relation; the self is not the relation but is the relation's relating itself to itself. A human being is a synthesis of the infinite and the finite, of the temporal and the eternal, of freedom and necessity, in short, a synthesis. A synthesis is a

relation between two. Considered in this way, a human being is still not a self (*Ibid.*, p. 351).

Is that clear?! To Anti-Climacus the self is, above all, spirit, but that is best understood by seeing that the self is from one perspective a dynamic duality, a blended, reciprocating synthesis whose dimensions provide for interaction and vital intercourse with each other, a synthesis always relating itself to itself. From this perspective the self is merely a synthesis, akin to the mind-body duality. However, in this case the synthesis is also defined in sets of intimately related but intellectually opposing dimensions represented in abstract categories of the mind that cover everything from the finite to the infinite, the temporal to the eternal, and from states of freedom to those of necessity. The scope of the self as a mental and emotional synthesis embraces these domains.

As such, the self is just that, a synthesis of two, a negative, static, but related unity. This relation, or better, the movement of relating itself to itself, constitutes a third dimension to which the synthesis relates, and in this added dimension may also relate itself to another—but only with the advent and aid of spirit. If so, it is now related dynamically in a new and positive relationship—and this is the "authentic" self! (Compare this use of "synthesis" with that of Hegel.) But here we return to the theme of despair.

According to Anti-Climacus, the self either brought itself about or it was established by some other force or power. If it was created by another power, then this becomes an added relationship, that is, a relation to that which established the self. In that case the authentic self is derived—a dynamic, synthetic unity that relates itself to itself, and in relating and existing thus, relates to a power sufficient to establish it. And here is where despair, echoing Judge William, returns. If the self established itself, despair takes the form of a person (like the "young man") unwilling to be oneself; but if the self is derived, established by another power, despair has the form of willing to be oneself. For the self to imagine it can resolve this by itself and to be rid of despair results in a mis-relationship, a faulty assumption, and misreading by an unauthentic self. If and when despair is rooted out, according to Anti-Climacus, the case is that in relating itself to itself and in willing to be oneself, the authentic self is grounded transparently—as in a mirror darkly—in the eternal power, the supernatural force that created it. It is a glimpse of man's "eternal validity."

In short, the self is not just an object of reality that is defined by observing human behavior from without, "objectively;" observed from within, "subjectively," it is, as we shall see, a complex reality all its own!

Such, according to Anti-Climacus, is the nature of the self. But there is much more about this nature in Kierkegaard's or his pseudonyms' penetrating views on inwardness and subjectivity—a topic noted first in *The Concept of Irony*—in what follows.

SUBJECTIVITY

We should consider first what we think "reality" is and how to have reliable knowledge of it, that is, the "truth."

Typically we rely on our senses initially to give us knowledge of our surroundings by hearing, seeing, smelling, tasting, and touching. The impressions and images they provide flood in on us as if, according to the English philosopher and statesman John Locke (1632-1704), they imprint the recipient mind, a *tabula rasa* or blank tablet, from birth. The mind then sorts and classifies the sounds, sights, odors, and so forth into concepts or ideas which are stored and named for recall in memory. Without the work of the mind, objects and forces that cause or bring about experience or awareness of this kind of reality would lie outside us. And this is the external world, outwardness (a somewhat awkward expression of it), or "objectivity."

Now consider also the breadth of experience we ascribe peculiarly to the self and its form of "awareness:" self-consciousness, -confidence, -reliance, -assuredness, -worth, -doubt, -preservation, -absorption, -realization, -love, selfishness, and the like. Then there are the accompanying feelings and emotions to which we give names like despair, anxiety, fear, dread, hope, love, trust, regret, guilt, elation, and others. And this is the internal world, inwardness, or "subjectivity." Is this kind of experience any less real or true than the external world?

As ways of knowing, however, subjectivity and objectivity are commonly regarded as polar opposites. The former, relating to the subject, the knowing person, is thought by some to be inferior to the latter, less reliable, because it comes from a source not given to direct observation by others for verification. It is the notion that what is external to the subject, the world of objects, should be known dispassionately, unbiased, independently verified, based on the principles and methods of scientific observation and hypothesis.

While Kierkegaard does not deny or disparage the presumed objectivity of science for its usefulness in extracting from perception and thought the multiple laws that seem to govern the world around us, he would argue also that, like Socrates, knowledge of the self by deep introspection can be equally valid, and that the characterization of human subjects solely by deduction from the external, objective observation of personal behavior is far from sufficient knowledge of existence. Personal reality, he believed, is best discerned by the subject, inwardly and subjectively.

Right or wrong, Søren Kierkegaard chose it as his model, and he did so specifically in Johannes Climacus' *Philosophical Fragments* and finally—the last and most extensive book Kierkegaard thought he would write, by the same pseudonym—*The Concluding Unscientific Postscript to the Philosophical Fragments*.

In the first book, Climacus focuses his attention on Socrates, as developed in several of Plato's *Dialogues* but mainly in the *Meno* beginning with the question whether the truth can be learned. To Socrates,

> a person cannot possibly seek what he knows, and just as impossibly, he cannot seek what he does not know, for what he knows he cannot seek, since he knows it, and what he does not know he cannot seek, because, after all, he does not even know what he is supposed to seek. Socrates thinks through the difficulty by means [of the principle] that all learning and seeking are but recollecting. Thus the ignorant

person merely needs to be reminded in order, by himself, to call to mind what he knows. The truth is not introduced into him but was in him. Socrates elaborates on this idea, and in it the Greek pathos is in fact concentrated, since it later becomes a demonstration for the immortality of the soul— retrogressively, please note—or a demonstration for the pre-existence of the soul (*Ibid.*, p. 117).

The argument validates Socrates' method of examining the unacceptable or poorly reasoned opinions of those he encountered in the Athenian marketplace. He likened himself to a midwife ("maieutic" denotes the same) who helps a pregnant woman deliver a healthy child. To scrutinize one's assumptions is essential if for no other reason than to discover that the exercise of one's clearest and most exacting reflection is therefore the surest form of understanding. As the *Dialogues* suggest, fundamental ignorance can be relieved by recollecting what must always have been known. As one way of putting it, the truth is "immanent" in one's own mental resources. And, as Climacus notes, between one person and another, the means Socrates used to elicit the truth from himself and others is perhaps the highest form of knowledge. (Note "recollection" from *The Stages*.)

But what, asks Climacus, if Socrates (or Plato) is wrong? In that case a person is not where the truth is, nor is the truth in the person, so that it has to be given from outside oneself, revealed in some external manner. Thus the person is so confused that not only is one ignorant of the truth but is looking in the wrong direction to find it. That means one has lost the condition, the capacity for knowing it, by virtue of one's own misguided character. To put it in ethico-religious terms, the person is guilty, and, says Climacus, we should call this present condition, "sin"—a term which most persons would recognize, though they may not understand it or apply it to themselves.

What Climacus has done is to replace the Greek categories with known religious ones—and to replace Socrates with Jesus, though unnamed. Climacus continues by noting that the person in this condition would therefore need a teacher who is capable of giving one both the truth and the condition for understanding it. This teacher would change the person, transform him/her in readiness to receive the truth. But of course no ordinary teacher can do this, muses Climacus; it would have to be God. And because a person is a prisoner to one's ignorant, guilty, and helpless state, this godly teacher alone can liberate, redeem, and save the person—an act that places one so much in debt that it becomes a trust for which one must forever care.

Thus Climacus, from an academic, not a personally religious standpoint, explores the difference between the Socratic (or Platonic) claim to immanent, recollected truth by way of self-examination, and the religious, near-Christian view of a transcendent source for the truth of the human condition. It is an hypothesis wrapped in a philosophical and historical discussion of Socrates and other Greek thinkers, which then becomes more revealing as Climacus dramatizes his theory with a kind of parable. It recounts the story of the love of a king for a humble maiden. Reflecting the belief in the doctrine of the incarnation, it suggests that the king, like God, took the part of a commoner, knowing that if he meant to win her love, he must humble himself before her, even take on the appearance of a servant:

> But this servant-form is no mere outer garment, like the king's beggar cloth which thus flutters loosely about him and betrays the king; it is not like the filmy summer cloak of Socrates, which though woven of nothing yet both conceals and reveals. It is his true form and figure. For this is the unfathomable nature of love, that it desires equality with the beloved, not in jest but in earnest and in truth and

so that God must suffer all things, endure all things, experience all things absolutely like the humblest—behold the man! (from a translation by Reidar Thomte).

Climacus, always the academic but with a particular interest in a religion like Christianity, crowns this work (late in Kierkegaard's authorship) with a major "postscript," *The Concluding Unscientific Postscript to the Philosophical Fragments*. He makes it clear, however, that he is not as interested in the validity or truth of a religion like Christianity as he is in the individual's relation to it. The issue for him, first stated in the introduction to the *Fragments*, is this: "Can a historical point of departure be given for an eternal consciousness; how can such a point of departure be of more than historical interest; can an eternal happiness be built on historical knowledge?" To theologians such questions are means for explaining the nature and truths of religion as presented for example in its edifices, scriptures, doctrines, and creeds. To Climacus the issue is this, as if hypothetically he himself were to commit to it:

> I, Johannes Climacus, born and bred in this city and now thirty years old, an ordinary human being like most folk, assume that a highest good, called an eternal happiness, awaits me just as it awaits a housemaid and a professor. I have heard that Christianity is one's prerequisite for this good. I now ask how I may enter into relation to this doctrine (*TEK*, op. cit. p. 189f.).

A highest good? Climacus has barely hidden, though borrowed from, ethico-religious language. To Kant, for example, the highest good is a happiness achieved by adhering to the universal imperative: always at least to intend to act in such a way that one's action is reasonably consistent with what is right and just for everyone everywhere. To Aristotle, following Plato, the highest good as developed in his book,

The Nichomachean Ethics, is a happiness achieved by embodying what he called the "Golden Mean." It requires that one always choose a course of action between the extremes of present choices, neither the excessive nor the deficient, nothing too much or too little.

The idea is to choose the middle way, habitually, until it becomes second nature to do what is ethical or of good character, which is the same. For example, the courageous person is neither foolhardy nor cowardly, and to take that "middle way" also goes for several of the traits we most admire and that constitute one's ethical character.

Of course what precisely the highest good is, is therefore relative to the individual and one's situation. Why? Because what is excessive to one may be somewhat deficient to another; there is no absolute rule except to personally identify and maximize the Mean. By doing so consistently, one establishes a lifelong pattern for achieving the highest mortal happiness the ethical life can achieve. So, as many other ethicists like Mill and Kant have theorized, Climacus wants to know how the highest good, happiness—a happiness of a sort that is lasting and which many religions promise their adherents—can be achieved.

Eduard Geismar saw the *Postscript*, which presumably spans the whole realm of human subjectivity, as centering on a major challenge to Climacus' ethical idealism.

> We must start with the ethical ideal as it exists for the individual. Ethics requires of each man that he give his entire attention to the discovery and development of his moral possibilities. In this concern for himself he becomes more and more subjective; the [speculative] philosophical way of greater and greater objectivity is the way of greater and greater absent-mindedness, leading farther and farther away from the self. The *Unscientific Postscript* develops the theme that Ethics would despair of achieving any

foothold whatever in human life, if it were not the case that the highest task set for every human being is to become subjective. Kierkegaard's thought is through and through idealistic.

Given Anti-Climacus' analysis in *The Sickess Unto Death* that the self is a synthesis of the temporal and eternal, the eternal is not some speculative concept but it "wears the aspect of futurity, and revealed itself as something that comes to be. In the moment of decision, the eternal is the future. Such is the primary and fundamental paradox of human existence" (*Lectures on the Religious Thought of Søren Kierkegaard*, Eduard Geismar, Augsburg Publishing House, 1937, p. 46f.).

One might here recall the suspension and profound questioning of ethical idealism in Johannes de Silentio's *Fear and Trembling*. It is the dramatic description of the paradoxes entailed by God's command to Abraham to sacrifice—murder—Isaac, together with the impossibility turned miracle that restored or reduplicated all to Abraham and Sarah. In fact, to Geismar the issue is also linked to Constantine's *Repetition* where the "young man" is faced with the possibility of a repetition, a reduplication of his existence to become himself once again, but as a wholly new person.

> His thought will reflect his own situation in existence, with its contrary poles: subjective conviction and objective uncertainty. But what will a man's existence be like if he submits himself to the ethical ideal and his life to the law of reduplication? According to the *Postscript* it will be describable in terms of three life-long disciplines. These are: first, an absolute commitment to the highest end; second, an essential acceptance of the discipline of suffering; third, an interpenetration of the consciousness with the sense of guilt (*Ibid.*, p. 48f.).

In short, it is Søren Kierkegaard's prelude to the possibility and need to become religious. We will say more about these "disciplines" later.

As an underlying theme Climacus is once again concerned about the difference between objectivity and subjectivity. They both claim truth, but in different ways. The objective claim is based on knowledge gleaned from observation, and with the help of inductive logic and mathematics will include historical research and theoretical science; subjective truth is, as the Kierkegaard literature amply describes, the stuff of personal existence, inwardness, passions, self-conscious reflection, decisiveness, and freedom of the will. Religious doctrines may be logically justifiable, backed by extensive historical insight, and the authenticity of its Scriptures. But is one's commitment to such truths sufficient and efficacious to achieve the highest good, to warrant eternal happiness? Or does it take passions like personal integrity, care of one's neighbor, truthful insight into the human self, or trust—subjective qualities?

Climacus understands very well that his position is regarded as "unscientific." To him the conclusion is clear: neither historically nor speculatively can one gather the kind of evidence that would rationally or scientifically prove with certainty either the existence of God or the validity of a Christian life, or any other comparable religious view. He might have noted that many great thinkers have tried impressively, persuasively, to prove the existence of God—scholars such as St. Anselm (1033-1109) in his *Proslogion*, and Blaise Pascal (1623-1662) in his *Pensees*. Ironically, they failed to be very effective—not because their proofs were logically invalid, but because such proof is rarely if ever sufficient to move people, to overcome or change a person's deeply felt views.

Apparently, Climacus concludes from his study, to be a religious believer requires a kind of ultimate passion, a "leap," a risk and challenge to intellectual, scientific, and objective perspectives—a commitment that nonetheless one subjectively knows to be true. The truth he has in mind is not amenable to historical or speculative findings, and its definition is actually a paraphrase for faith. He writes:

> Faith is the contradiction between the infinite passion of inwardness and the objective uncertainty. If I am able to apprehend God objectively, I do not have faith; but because I cannot do this, I must have faith. If I want to keep myself in faith, I must continually see to it that I hold fast the objective uncertainty, see to it that in the objective uncertainty I am "out on 70,000 fathoms of water" and still have faith. The thesis that subjectivity, inwardness, is truth contains the Socratic wisdom, the undying merit of which is to have paid attention to the essential meaning of existing, [that the knower is] an existing person. That is why, in his ignorance, Socrates was in the truth in the highest sense within paganism. To comprehend this, that the misfortune of speculative thought is simply that it forgets again and again that the knower is an existing person, can already be rather difficult in our objective age. "But [as I've said in the *Fragments*] to go beyond Socrates when one has not even comprehended the Socratic— that, at least, is not Socratic" (*TEK*, op. cit., p. 207).

In the human condition, Socratic ignorance is truth.

At this point Climacus, like de Silentio in *Fear and Trembling*, introduces again the idea of the paradox, the ultimate obstacle to rational thought:

> When subjectivity, inwardness, is truth, then truth, objectively defined, is a paradox; and that truth is objectively a paradox shows precisely that subjectivity is truth. The paradox is the objective uncertainty that is the expression for the passion of inwardness that is truth. So much for the Socratic. The eternal,

essential truth, that is, the truth that is related essentially to the existing person by pertaining essentially to what it means to exist is a paradox (*Ibid.*, p. 208).

For Climacus, Socrates remains the consummate ironist.

That may be enough for Johannes Climacus, subjectivity, and Socratic truth. It serves to introduce Søren Kierkegaard's remaining pseudonymous work to the next existential dimension: what it means to be religious.

RELIGIOUSNESS

After the somewhat taxing analyses in the foregoing, a brief review may be in order.

In his effort, like that of Socrates, to explore and understand the human condition inwardly and what it means to exist, Kierkegaard begins by establishing the fundamental insight into human despair, which then his pseudonymous authors trace through stages or modes of life identified as esthetic, ethical, and religious. As we shall see, they are linked as well with intermediate dimensions labeled as "irony" (between the esthetic and the ethical) and "humor" (between the ethical and the religious).

The esthetic mode is defined as the despair that reveals itself in not being willing to recognize or be oneself, one's original self. The ethical mode is declared to be the despair that comes at willfully trying to be a better but still despairing self, only to discover that for all one's good intentions, despair cannot be rooted out by ethical effort alone. The human condition is too flawed, too complex to enable it. What one needs to understand is that the self is a dynamic synthesis of body, mind, and, above all, spirit. It is a reciprocating relationship that in relating itself to itself, relates itself to another, that is, to a power capable of bringing the authentic self into being, capable of transforming, redeeming the self by overcoming despair and giving it a presentiment of its eternal validity. It is just a hint of the supernatural, little more than that except for the sense that one is dependent on some higher power for one's authentic self to be what it is. And this for Kierkegaard approaches the religious levels of existence, two of them, for a new and final pseudonymous expression.

At the age of thirty-three Kierkegaard (as Johannes Climacus) wrote the *Postscript* in the belief that it would be his last publication before his death. In fact, though his health was in decline, he lived another nine years. In that time he continued his feverish output of works with new pseudonyms as well as discourses under his own name, all increasingly devoted to the categories of religiosity, or better, "religiousness." Up to this point in his authorship the idea of religion is to be understood rather broadly, not yet in specifically Christian terms. Kierkegaard's plan is to introduce the religious or (a somewhat awkward term) religiousness step by step. However it is hardly necessary for readers to be religious in order to understand or appreciate the plan.

For example, Climacus' position in the *Fragments* and its immense *Postscript* are academic, psychical, philosophical inquiries into the nature of religion, not in Kierkegaard's view the highest expression of it. To Climacus, it is presented on two levels, "A" and "B."

"A" can be viewed as the kind of religion developed out of one's own experience, and mental and emotional resources. It has the character of a "search for meaning in life" and perhaps for some higher, otherworldly, and presumably benevolent power that would serve to make existence somewhat more tolerable and meaningful in the face of common despair. It would preserve one's personal dignity despite the occasional experiences of resignation over the fateful way things happen, over one's various kinds of suffering, and with guilt for not having acted otherwise. Such patterns are amply reflected in classical Greek tragedies like Aeschylus' *Agamemnon* or Sophocles' *Antigone* in Socrates' time.

At this level of religiousness, one may have an intimation and vague conception of a supernatural being sufficiently powerful to create and sustain the universe, though perhaps a force either powerless or unwilling to rid the world of its seemingly mindless catastrophes. If the view exacts some "consciousness of guilt" in the person for the memory of wrongs he or she committed in the past, it need not be understood only in religious terms. As we have seen in Anti-Climacus' *Sickness*, guilt is the ultimate form of the despairing self, the sense that something is deeply wrong with the human condition, something that without divine assistance cannot be excised.

Again, religiousness "A" might be embodied in those who virtually identify the supernatural with Mother Nature, or who seek peace of mind in meditation with unknown but hopefully healing forces. As we will see in a later section describing Kierkegaard's "right-handed" writings, religiousness "A" is often the subject of the need for "edification" that is both consoling and enlightening. In any case, "A" is far-reaching in its varied appeal to humanity, an appeal that resonates within the bounds of fundamentally human curiosity, capacity, and the search for meaning in life.

Religiousness "B" represents a specifically new and superior dimension of existence governed by divine action. Some of this of course is approached in the *Fragments* where, contrary to the view of the immanent knowledge or recollection in Socrates' view, the truth one seeks is not elicited from within but is conveyed from without by divine intervention in human affairs. It rather transparently compares the difference by introducing the unnamed Jesus, the incarnate God, as the one who can convey not only the true meaning in life, but also the condition for receiving it. Additional hints of religiousness are recognized in Constantine's use of the story of Job in *Repetition* and in de Silentio's dramatic telling of the story of Abraham and Isaac in *Fear and Trembling*. However, it should be remembered that they suggest religiousness "A," not "B."

This is perhaps the point at which to briefly explain also Kierkegaard's interest in two intermediate domains of existence, "irony" and "humor." The former rests uneasily between the esthetic and ethical modes, and the latter somewhere between the ethical and religious positions. As Kierkegaard apparently learned from his dissertation topic, *The Concept of Irony, with Continual Reference to Socrates*, the legendary Athenian is the embodiment of irony because he is depicted as ignorant when all his followers, though not his detractors, agreed he was truly wise. As the term implies, the irony lies in the notion that ignorance is in fact wisdom, its contrary. For Kierkegaard, irony suggests a kind of existence opposed to the esthetic but not decisively ready yet to adopt the ethical; it represents no specific point of view but is rather embodied in Socrates' self-searching manner.

Humor is similarly disposed in the person who, like Johannes Climacus (and contrary to Kant), regards the ethical quest for moral goodness to be doomed and therefore profoundly comical. He is unable to move either way, and he knows it. Thus, he can be little more than academic about his interest in religion, though he appreciates what it takes to appropriate it, to make a religiousness like "A" his own. By the way, Kierkegaard thought Hamann, Kant's contemporary critic, represented the ultimate humorist.

Perhaps the best and most explicit of Søren Kierkegaard's works for representing "B," now revealed as Christianity, is *Practice in Christianity* by the pseudonym Anti-Climacus. He, you will recall, is also the author of *The Sickness Unto Death*, though Kierkegaard is named as the editor of both, a hint perhaps that he is becoming less secretive about his writings. Anti-Climacus is much more forthcoming than Johannes about what in his judgment authentic religiousness requires of a person. Johannes' view may allude to the nature of Christianity, but only, Anti-Climacus would say, if it is represented with the highest possible standards—standards regarded as excessive and unduly critical by Danish Church leaders near the end of Kierkegaard's life, as we shall see.

Practice is uncommonly insistent and uncompromising in its view that Jesus is, as the New Testament scriptures variously record it, the Way, the Truth, and the Life. He is the incarnate God, the enactment of God's will for the nature and purpose of human existence. As the "God-man," Jesus is the epitome of the paradox, and as such the ultimate "offense" to perception, logic, and rationality. Anti-Climacus writes:

> Just as the concept "faith" is an altogether distinctively Christian term, so in turn is "offense" an altogether distinctively Christian term relating to faith. The possibility of offense is the crossroad, or it is like standing at the crossroad. From the possibility of offense, one turns either to offense or to faith, but one never comes to faith except from the possibility of offense. Essentially offense is related to the composite of God and man, or to the God-man. [S]peculation takes away from the God-man the qualifications of temporality, contemporaneity and actuality. On the whole it is tragic that this has been feted as profundity—No, the *situation* belongs with the God-man that an individual human being who is standing beside you is the God-man. The God-man is not the union of God and man. The God-man is the unity of God and an individual human being. That the human race is supposed to be in kinship with God is ancient paganism, but *that* an individual human being is God is Christianity" (*Ibid.*, p. 373f.).

To Anti-Climacus, offense takes two forms, either by considering the God-man's loftiness, His Highness, as an individual human being who claims to be God; or by noting the lowliness, the humility of a God who is a human being. One will be offended that any person claims to be God, and also offended that God is said to be a man. "The God-man is the paradox, absolutely the paradox. Therefore, it is altogether certain that the understanding must come to a standstill on it {and] Christ himself warns against offense" (*Ibid.*, p. 375).

Thus, practice or training to be a Christian must necessarily result in the possibility of offense. So imagine, notes Anti-Climacus, how it all could affect a child (apparently a boy). Suppose one begins by showing the child a picture of Napoleon, a great leader astride his horse; then perhaps one of William Tell with the story of his fearful need to shoot an arrow at an apple on the head of his beloved young son. Finally one shows the child a picture of a man who is being crucified on a large wooden cross, a most painful way to die, reserved for the worst criminals long ago. The spiteful placard on the cross says the man is "King of the Jews."

What will the child think? Will the picture ever be forgotten? What, the child may ask, did this man do to deserve this death?

> See, now is the moment; if you have not already made too powerful an impression upon the child, tell him now about the one who was lifted up, who from on high will draw all to himself, this crucified man. Tell the child that he was love, that he came to the world out of love, took upon himself the form of a lowly servant, lived for only one thing—to love and to help people, especially all those who were sick and sorrowful and suffering and unhappy (*Ibid.*, p. 376f.).

Anti-Climacus goes on to intensify the story by telling the child about the man's betrayal and condemnation, even as the robber on a cross beside him was set free by the blindly hate-filled crowd below. Then tell the child the rest of the story, the agony of the crucified one who cries to God for release from this fate, but who, accepting it, experiences an amazing resurrection after his death. Is there any reasonable motivation for the child as he grows up, to want to follow in this man's footsteps?

At this point Anti-Climacus directs his attention to the Church at large. "In Christendom, sermons, lectures, and speeches are heard often enough about what is required of an imitator of Christ, what it means to follow Christ, etc. [O]nly by listening more closely does one discover a deeply hidden, un-Christian, basic confusion and dubiousness. The Christian sermon today has become mainly 'observations'" (*Ibid.*, p. 378). Unfortunately, he points out, they can too often be objective, dispassionate, impersonal comments that distance hearers from the real point, namely to imitate Christ, a truth that must be reflected inwardly. Therefore, "it is a risk to preach, for as I go up into that holy place—whether the church is packed or as good as empty, whether I myself am aware of it or not, I have one listener, God in heaven whom I certainly cannot see but who truly can see me" (*Ibid.*, p. 379). It is one thing to be an observer, a commentator or admirer, but quite another to be an "imitator."

The *Practice* develops the recurring and uncompromising theme that to be Christian is, in effect, to be contemporary with Christ, to always imitate him as the "prototype" of human existence regardless of the offensiveness to good sense it may cause. In that respect Anti-Climacus imagines the reactions that various types of persons might have, such as the church pastor, the philosopher, the statesman, the skeptic, the leading citizen—each with objections of one sort or another about the God-man's appearance, personality, or pronouncements. In response, Anti-Climacus reminds each observer of Christ's admonition, "Blessed is the person who takes no offense at me."

In Kierkegaard's final years he quarreled publicly in published letters and pamphlets with highly-regarded leaders of the Danish Church. Generally, he accused them of failing to present the Christian religion in ways that underscore the suffering, humiliation, and offense that are central to Christ's life and teachings. Instead, he suggested, the Church seems to want to go with the flow, to make people comfortable, and to do whatever is expedient to avoid the inevitable conflicts that characterize cultural change.

Thus, where in religiousness "A" one may live with unrequited despair, a consciousness of guilt for wrongdoing, and an intimation of the existence of the supernatural, in religiousness "B" the fundamental condition for faith in relation to offense is a consciousness of sin, the ultimate flaw in the human self. "B" assumes, moreover, that only God can reveal this, and to experience forgiveness for it is to become, as the "young man" discovered in *Repetition*, an essentially new person.

Finally, Anti-Climacus presents his position in an imagined conversation with a mocker:

> And the mocker who is admired by all for his wit and liked for his good nature might say—"After all, that is a priceless idea that an individual man, just like the rest of us, says that he is God. If that is not to confer a benefit upon men, I do not know what benevolence and beneficence can mean! Given that the criterion for being God is that it is just to look like all the rest of us, tomorrow I shall proclaim that I, the undersigned, am God—and the one who realizes this cannot deny it without contradicting oneself."

But then Anti-Climacus responds:

> True, there was nothing about him that we should admire, nothing to be seen but a lowly man who, by signs and wonders and affirming that he was God, continually posited the possibility of offense. Indeed, if any person possessed all human wisdom and shrewdness along with all human talents, it would profit one little. Christianity shall in a degree corresponding to one's superiority erect itself against one,

and transform itself into madness and terror, until one learns either to give up Christianity, or else by the help of what is [beyond logical and historical proofs], that is, by the help of the torments of a contrite heart one learns to enter by the narrow way, through the consciousness of sin, into Christianity.

(The two quotes above are from personal notes; the translator is unidentified.)

Next, no overview of Kierkegaard's life and writings is adequate without some description of his extensive and parallel "right-handed" authorship, the works under his own name, not pseudonyms. That is the task that follows.

DISCOURSE

As uncompromising as Anti-Climacus' *Practice* is, Søren Kierkegaard makes no claim to have inwardly, personally achieved its requirements. His task only is to allow the author to set Christianity's standards as high as possible, though he is willing to be the work's editor. However, he is not bashful about assuming the credit for a large number of complementary essays and *Edifying Discourses* written during the same period as the pseudonymous authorship.

As the title suggests they are discourses designed to be uplifting, suitable for edification, even quasi-devotional in tenor. The somewhat awkward but accurate term "ethico-religious" has been coined to describe their character. Kierkegaard is appealing to readers who might naturally expect a literature that is inspirational, high-minded, and that challenges one to consider indirectly what an ethical, even religious way of life might require. With some notable exceptions the discourses presuppose a climate in which religion is mainly regarded as immanent, not transcendent, but of human creativity and imagination. They are upbuilding in that the reader is urged to change, to improve one's outlook on life. We must also excuse Kierkegaard for his nearly exclusive use of the masculine gender in nouns and pronouns that refer to human beings. He clearly intends no anti-feminism, rather merely a use that reflects a universal sense of mankind, humanity, etc.

Because Kierkegaard emphasizes so strongly the place of "suffering" in life, perhaps an early description of the group of discourses under the title *The Gospel of Suffering* is an appropriate place to start. It is not Søren Kierkegaard's title but is the third section of the *Edifying Discourses* and first translated by David F. Swenson (Augsburg Publishing House, 1947).

Collected under the title, each discourse of *Gospel*, with a hint of the paradoxical, juxtaposes suffering with joy, though each discourse takes a different scriptural point of departure using striking pronouncements from the record of Jesus' life. To many readers, who may not necessarily be religious, Jesus might at the very least represent the universal model of the upright, ethical life.

The first discourse begins with the familiar theme reflected in the *Practice* that to "imitate" Jesus is, in a metaphorical sense, to take up his cross and be prepared to suffer—to bear the humiliation, offensiveness, self-denial, and loneliness which also may be expected of one who must one day answer to God for one's actions on earth. Still, there is a joy or longed-for happiness in this, like that of the child who for the first time walks by oneself, though afterward in life experiences the manifold setbacks to happiness. Lasting joy or happiness offered at its highest level is more than a hope; it is a Godly promise awaiting the imitator of Jesus.

The discourses that follow continue the theme of joy in suffering, for example, how it is that one's burdens can seem light though one's suffering is heavy. The relationship of man to God in the figure of Jesus is also a pattern of human existence, of the link of eternal validity between the human self and the supernatural. Suffering is pervasive, relentless, and painful, and for most a daily challenge to personal resourcefulness. But, Kierkegaard suggests, faith in God is more powerful, a surprising kind of transformation of suffering that is experienced when humanly matched with the meekness and humbleness so profoundly evident in Jesus' life.

Perhaps the third of the pieces does better justice to the theme of suffering. It is the joy or happiness in knowing that the school of suffering, its educational program, trains for eternity. As young people think about what they might want most out of life, there might be one of them who chose what promises to challenge and inspire, despite its dangers and hardships. It would not occur to this person to choose suffering, of course, unless one's purpose somehow was to model one's life after Jesus and, in so doing, learn the lessons of human anguish and despair. Kierkegaard notes that there is a kind of wisdom that comes from suffering, though most people would want to know how that can be when the experience of suffering itself is quite enough.

Though Jesus, who claimed to be God, was profoundly humbled and obliged to suffer at the cruel hands of detractors, he learned obedience. For a person, that is not easy, and is contrary to most kinds of learning. For if Jesus is also God, who must know all things but yet learned from obedience, it means there must be important lessons to be learned from suffering the hateful words and acts he knew at the hands of others, and from the nature of human existence itself. A guilt-ridden person has no reason to lose faith in God, but an innocent person like Jesus must somehow learn from one's sufferings. What do they teach?

Kierkegaard writes, suffering

> directs a man's attention *inward.* If that succeeds, the man will not despairingly resist it, seek to drown himself and to forget it in worldly diversions, in amazing undertakings, in comprehensive, indifferent knowledge—if it succeeds, then the instruction in it begins for it is in the inward man where suffering instructs, where God is listening, where obedience is the test which is demanded. Suffering indeed frequently comes from without, but it is only when the suffering is assimilated in the inner man that the instruction begins (Geismar, op. cit. p. 55).

Suffering essentially enables one to learn about oneself and one's relationship to God; in that respect, suffering is an indication that one is being instructed, schooled for eternity.

Then with a nod to the *Fragments*, Kierkegaard says that the instruction is not a matter of self-knowledge alone; God is the teacher. In the school of suffering, one must let God rule in everything; in obedience there is consolation in the thought of eventual eternal happiness, the everlasting truth for the person who aspires to it. In this school the joy comes when the learner, accepting and obedient to one's sufferings, is fundamentally changed—a new person—even as Jesus in his debasement humbled himself and became obedient in order to train every person for eternity.

Kierkegaard follows up this theme with similar discourses intended to be parallel or complementary to the pseudonymous works like *Fragments* and *Postscript*—themes such as: the joy, perplexing to humans, in knowing that in relation to God a person always suffers as being guilty; or in the thought that it is not the way which is narrow but the narrowness which is the way; and others. With sparing use of theological concepts and doctrines except for the references to God and the familiar notions of guilt and sin, Kierkegaard dialectically examines the ethico-religious dimension. He writes in ways that challenge and lay bare the search for meaning in life, particularly the prospects of ultimate and transforming relief from the essential and unending experience of human suffering.

Almost always, the point of departure for each discourse is common experience eventually elevated to the higher, ethico-religious plane. Actually, the *Edifying Discourses* lead off with a section to remind the reader of what is required to be an ethical person. In a group once entitled as *Purity of Heart*, the task of an ethical individual is to will one and only one thing, and that is to achieve "the good," a person's highest perfection, and this only when it is pursued decisively, honestly.

Kierkegaard treats the good as an ideal approaching the Platonic search in the *Stages:*

> To will one thing cannot mean to will something that only seemingly is one thing. Indeed, what else is desire in its boundless extreme but nausea? What else is earthly honor at its dizzy summit but contempt for existence? . . . Only the good is one thing in its essence and the same in every one of its expressions. But neither is willing one thing *that drastic error of presumptuous, ungodly enthusiasm: to will the great, no matter whether it is good or evil.* Holy Scripture teaches for our salvation that sin is a human being's corruption and therefore deliverance is only in purity through willing the good. But even if the good man lived in an out-of-way place in the world and never saw anyone else, he is still at one with himself and at once one with all, because he wills one thing and because the good is one thing (*TEK*, op. cit., pp. 271-275).

This is perhaps a good example of ethico-religious writing.

However, Geismar likes the discourse on another theme, one of Kierkegaard's earliest, namely, that "man's need of God is his highest perfection." It foresees the nature and failure of human striving to will the good. Granted this relationship to God may be a stretch for Søren Kierkegaard's readers, yet by viewing a person's perfection in this way one learns also to know oneself. If one fails to know oneself, life is said to be a delusion, an inability to reckon with the difference between the "inner" and the "outer" self. The latter seeks naively to get its satisfactions in life by virtue of its own mental and physical resources; the former, the deeper self, truly understands that it can gain no lasting satisfaction without God. These two selves vie with each other for primacy (a hint, perhaps of Kant's duality of the self): the outer self makes plans and devises strategies for achieving as near as possible its desires; the inner self "points to the uncertainty that attaches to all such calculations, immovably standing by its imperturbable 'perhaps;' and it thus prevents the outer self from moving to realize its ambitions" (Geismar, op. cit., p. 65f.).

With an analogy he also used to characterize the breach with the ethical in *Fear and Trembling*, Kierkegaard likens the superiority of the inner self over the outer self to the weaning of a child. It brings about a measure of self-denial and suffering for the child, but it is a matter of growing up. The outer self will always aspire to its objectives in the external world, but above all in its realization that one's need for God is the highest attainable achievement.

Related somewhat to the latter is another section of the edifying or upbuilding discourses that comprises three pieces devoted to the need to be content in various respects with human existence as we should come to accept it. It is what we can learn from *The Lily in the Field and the Bird of the Air*. Among his most beautiful writings, Søren Kierkegaard regards the lilies and birds as teachers that in their way convey essential lessons of nature to mankind, such as silence, obedience, and happiness. It is hard, he notes, for humans to keep silent and thus lose one's precious moments of self-reflection. Silent in their beauty and view of things, and obedient to their unseen Creator, the flowers and birds can teach one to ponder respect—respect for a kind of suffering only exceeded by that of Jesus, and thus worthy to emulate. The lily and the bird are not given to the cares and worries common to humanity. They thrive in the silent expectation that their Maker will provide for their needs. As the words of Jesus make clear in the New Testament Gospel of Matthew, chapter 6, true contentment with one's existence comes from learning above all to seek first the realm of God.

Of course there is no adequate way that one can convey the lyrical beauty and deeply engaging, indirect or maieutic character of these discourses, except by reading them. Still, there are many other discourses to consider, though written with a somewhat different voice, in what follows.

CHANGE

A sense of change may be apparent in Kierkegaard's writings a year following the publication of the *Edifying Discourses*. It came with the publication of yet another extraordinary work in two volumes entitled *Works of Love*. As fate or fortune would have it, Kierkegaard had by this time become the subject of venomous criticism and parody from a popular but disreputable scandal sheet in Copenhagen calling itself the *Corsair*.

In a way that was characteristic of his own Socratic-like irony, Kierkegaard most likely triggered the affair by letting it be known that he was somewhat hurt and embarrassed that he alone among respectable citizens of Copenhagen had so far escaped the newspaper's taunts. The *Corsair* responded for months thereafter with scurrilous articles and drawings that cruelly caricatured among other things his physical appearance, leaving him at the mercy of jeering types who followed him as he walked the city's streets.

In one of his introductions to Søren Kierkegaard's writings, David Swenson suggests that it was a painful turning point in the ethico-religious authorship in which "the inner collision by which a man comes into collision with himself gives place to the external collision in which a man in pursuit of his duty, comes in conflict with environment," a conflict which makes one's duty a true act of self-denial (Swenson, *Edifying Discourses,* vol. II, p. xv, 77, Augsburg Publishing House, 1944). For Kierkegaard, the upshot was to express ever greater religious intensity in subsequent writings. The volumes on *Works of Love* and, in the same year, *Christian*

Discourses, seem to reflect this change. But the salient fact is that until this change, apparently Kierkegaard had never intended to write works including *Sickness* and *Practice* that employed such ethico-religious fervor.

In stark contrast to the esthetic preoccupations about love in the *Stages*, Kierkegaard warns that in no sense is the *Works* a dissertation on the concept or Platonic idea of love. Even love as we generally know it would presume to cover an inexhaustible and essentially inexpressible subject. Rather, this book purports merely to examine the "works" or acts of love. Most interpreters hold that it develops a social ethic based on Christianity, with a focus on the Golden Rule, perhaps, but more pointedly, Jesus' pronouncement that every person should love their neighbor as they love themselves. That is hardly a proposal for socialist government as we commonly define it, but it is a universal and imperative Christian ethic (to shadow Kant).

Kierkegaard opens the work by noting that every person is fearful of being deceived by something or someone, especially self-deception, but that is no reason to be fearful of or to resist love. Deception has a multitude of faces, and deception in love would hardly embrace them. On the contrary, to imagine that would be the clearest form of self-deception, for it would cheat a person of the opportunity to love. Know that whatever the nature of a person's experience in life, whatever happens, love abides.

Kierkegaard subtitled the work a "deliberation," as opposed to an edifying or upbuilding essay. The latter presupposes the reader's common understanding of the theme, but he/she lacks the new understanding which Kierkegaard intends to urge the reader to consider. A deliberation, presumably, is a much more aggressive and challenging discourse wherein the reader is assumed to hold or imagine a point of view totally contrary to the truth that Kierkegaard proposes. *Works of Love* examines in typically dialectical fashion the commandment to love your neighbor as truthfully and honestly as you love your own self. However, "self-love" is the principal impediment to this; by its nature it is forever drawn to attend to its own needs and desires before those of one's neighbor. Christianity abhors selfish love and abolishes it in favor of neighbor-love.

Kierkegaard goes on to set apart common notions of love such as erotic, spontaneous love, from love that is self-giving and unconditional—the kind transcendent in God's unceasing, unchanging love for mankind. It is, moreover, a duty to love in this manner—from God's point of view, you *shall* do it—since only then is love secured eternally, independently of human will and free from (an old nemesis) despair.

> Therefore love's commandment does not secure against despair by means of feeble, lukewarm grounds of comfort—that one must not take something too hard, etc. Indeed, is such a wretched sagacity, which "has ceased to sorrow," any less despair than the lover's despair; is it not rather an even worse kind of despair! No, love's commandment forbids despair—by commanding one to love.

Spontaneous or erotic love is mired in despair, which is manifest in unhappiness, painful experience, or emotional suffering. It is, to echo the *Sickness*, a mis-relationship in a person's innermost being, for "what makes a person despair is not misfortune but his lack of the eternal not to have undergone the change of eternity through duty's *shall*" (*TEK*, op. cit,. p. 291f.).

The section ends by turning to human love's way, though somewhat limited, of how it is, as represented in the Apostle Paul's well-known letter to the Corinthians, that a person's selfless love in fact is upbuilding, and as such does the same for the neighbor one loves. Later, Kierkegaard expands on the Pauline letter and especially the phrase, "love abides." Human patience is commendable, but love abides. Here Kierkegaard's emphasis is somewhat ethical by reference to the letter's pronouncement that among the great human acts of passion—faith, hope, and love—love is the greatest. Indeed, if a person experiences what he feels is its loss or change of heart, what he feels is not love, for love abides. That, akin to the "young man's" repetition, is the peculiar nature of love: what is otherwise lost to a person is lost; but love abides and is the changeless and eternal ground for reconciliation. (Note the Platonic-like ideality in the "abiding" nature of love.)

No further description of *Works of Love* will do justice to the work, perhaps one of Kierkegaard's most popular and engaging deliberations. It begs to be read.

Incredibly, in the same year as the publication of the *Works*, Kierkegaard produced another major series now collected under the title *Christian Discourses*. The first part considers the sort of troubles and cares that plague the pagan mind—the mind that is personally distant from God, lowly and despairing over his seemingly inferior status in life. The list of such troubles is imaginable—poverty, poor health, failure, and the like. What follows in a similar vein are topics relating to human suffering, the ineffectiveness of contemporary religion, and seven meditations on communion, the Christian rite based on Jesus' last supper with his apostolic followers.

In a familiar theme, Kierkegaard contrasts the lowly and their concerns with the lilies and the birds that have no cares. They are content with their existence and are anything but lowly in terms of self-worth; they are content to be simply what they are. Is there instruction in this? What the lowly person grieves and cares about is his lack of eminence, the absence of fulfillment. Still, in this state, the individual is not alone; as an individual from the very beginning he is what he is before God. In this respect, surprisingly, lowliness is eminence or greatness, since one is by nature beckoned forward in life by the Divine, the godly prototype of what it means to exist. In contrast, this is not the case with the pagan, who, without God and therefore not himself, sorrows that fate or destiny has left him without hope and deeply dissatisfied. His care is that he amounts to nothing when his only desire is to be someone, to be eminent in something, and so he despairs over his state. He has failed to know himself, to recognize what it is to be a human being, contrary to the lily or the bird, and so he fails most seriously to be a new person with a new way of life.

Once again using commonly opposing thoughts, Kierkegaard pleads that existence for the person who truly knows himself and recognizes his eternal validity, his link with eternity is such that, remarkably, adversity is in reality prosperity. Suffering is a persistent fact of life, but surprisingly is more life's goal than prosperity; the real goal is to turn one's self around. Adversity, suffering will lead one to this crucial point, that is, to seek first the kingdom of God. As Kierkegaard puts it, he who has suffered adversity has the task of renouncing what he feels he has been denied in life; and he who is prosperous, like the rich young ruler in the scriptural account, must renounce what he has been given. This, however, cannot be accomplished without the transcendent abolition of what stands in the way, that is, one's sinfulness—a corrupting but hidden condition of human existence that only God can displace. But know also, says Kierkegaard, that God understands this, knows the human heart, and is greater than its deepest imperfections.

With the approach to the consciousness of sin, Kierkegaard has introduced the ultimate condition for being religious, or religiousness "B." But then he backs off to allow the reader to reconsider what he may have begun to understand:

> So, then, adversity is prosperity. And you can very well understand it. You may, however, not really have faith that it is so. But (to offer you a little lighter

fare if the scriptural text about first seeking God's kingdom should be too strong for you) then do you believe that the poet, whose songs delight humankind, do you believe that he could have written these songs if adversity and hard sufferings had not been there to tune the soul! It is precisely in adversity, "when the heart sits in deepest gloom, then the harp of joy is tuned" (*TEK*, op. cit., p. 325).

Some interpreters of Kierkegaard sense that writings once published under the title *Thoughts on Crucial Situations in Human Life* really inaugurate his religious authorship in 1845. It is a collection of three meditations, each devoted to a significant and, in Kierkegaard's mind, crucial occasion; that is, one where decisiveness and change are necessary: the rites of confession ("What It Means to Seek God"), of marriage ("Love Conquers All"), and of burial ("The Decisiveness of Death"). If I were to choose one series that best elicits the major categories and emphases that introduce and succinctly point to Kierkegaard's religious intentions, this would be it.

In an order that reverses the progression of Kierkegaard's existential levels from the esthetic and ethical to the religious, the first discourse develops at length Johannes Climacus' distinctions between religiousness "A" and religiousness "B," but only after noting that what is decisive about their difference is the consciousness and confession of one's sins. It is a plea to look deeply into oneself, with a stillness that must not be disturbed lest one pass over or excuse before God the slightest fault or sense of a guilty conscience, the crucial element in religiousness "A."

It was said by Aristotle that philosophy begins in wonder. So too, says Kierkegaard, might a person naturally curious about the supernatural begin there—though Kierkegaard took his lead not from Aristotle but from the great Dutch philosopher Baruch Spinoza (1632-1677) and the latter's Jewish heritage of encounters with Jehovah. Kierkegaard explains that there are various levels of a consciousness of God, but all begin with wonder coupled with fear. At the most primitive level where the individual offers little or no imagination to his search for the supernatural, he is simply struck by the sheer uncertainty over what makes him fearful and curious about the ultimate origin and purpose of existence. Because he is caught up daily in the demands of self-preservation, he is not a serious "seeker," though he understands well the nature of danger and mystery. Wonder is most evident among young people; but whatever its nature, it is born in a stillness, a silence that is very personal, private, not something that can be shared. (This approaches the nature of confession.)

As he becomes more serious about things, the seeker's curiosity turns to a search in which he wishes that he could find and understand the supernatural. But he knows that, existentially speaking, he cannot. Still, even the consciousness of a feared and unknown God may evoke a kind of worshipful outlook in him drawn from the contemplation, for example, of puzzling and powerful forces of nature all around him. With this he is likely to become a pantheist—God is everywhere, in everything.

If this erstwhile seeker not only wishes but strives to find God, wonder diminishes, though striving can also lead to worship. But if in maturity he begins to feel he can find God on his own, wonder vanishes and is replaced by despair. He has begun in a new way to seek God, a sense of God approaching the religiousness of "A." He discovers that what he wants is within himself—immanent—though ill-identified except perhaps by his mixed emotions of fear and self-satisfaction over having located his sense of the supernatural. This sense is peculiarly his own and cannot be shared; it is learned in stillness before an omnipresent divinity.

Kierkegaard notes that it is obvious, therefore, that logical proofs for the existence of God are of no consequence. To a seeker whose principal desire is to know God, not just know something about God, his experience, that which governs the inner man, is accompanied by the lingering sense of fear, and his reason cannot explain what he knows either to himself or to others. Indeed, Kierkegaard remarks, it is a glimpse of what faith is like if one ultimately recognizes that the absolute wonder is God.

If the seeker once arrives at the point where he now assumes the existence of the supernatural, however that is defined for him, he is himself changed—and his inner self becomes the location where, he believes, God may truly exist. But having been changed, he finds that God is not there, and he is conscious instead of his own corrupt and sinful self, a consciousness so personal that one person cannot learn it from another. He can learn it only from a transcendent God who can convict him of his sin with a consciousness he must appropriate, make his own—and this, Kierkegaard reveals, is the crucial requirement for experiencing the true consciousness of God, namely, in religiousness "B" (and, we might add, *Practice in Christianity*).

The second discourse in the series, "On the Occasion of a Wedding," speaks to another crucial situation in life, but with an ethically prescriptive voice. It is somewhat akin to Judge William's advice to the despairing "young man" about the value and responsibilities of marriage in the second volume of *Either/Or*, though it may not quite reach the deliberative level of *The Works of Love*. Nonetheless, to expand in these modest reflections on the nature of a highly ethical union in which, as Kierkegaard's theme that "love conquers all" puts it here, may not add significantly to its appreciation. As a confessional in relation to a marriage, however, it is clearly well worth reading.

The third discourse reflects on what it is like, what goes through one's mind for a person to stand at a gravesite on the occasion of a funeral. It addresses the esthetic point of view, but "earnestly." A person cannot help but consider his own inevitable death—and also what he should make of his remaining life before death happens.

Standing at the gravesite when the funeral is over, there is no sound from the coffin; the deceased is silent and unable to respond to the brooding next-of-kin who "recollect" him now and on appropriately mindful occasions in the future. Nor does the deceased as far as we know recollect the mourners— or anything, not even God whom he faithfully recollected while he was living. In life he was respected, if obscure; a hard worker, a good citizen who sadly has left behind a grieving wife and family; they miss him terribly. Little will be said about him after the funeral; he died as he lived, quietly. However, in life and in all he accomplished, he recollected God. (Recall the concept.)

Returning from the funeral his family and friends in town may for an indefinite time recollect him, but he will not recollect them. He is gone forever, it is over—except for the earnestness with which the living resolve to understand the task which a death puts before them. It is not the frivolous shrug of resignation that says life is short, so make the best of it; it is rather the "earnestness" with which a person redirects and decisively empowers one's life to seize the opportunity to wonder at God, to escape the night of indifference and work while it is yet day.

The earnest person, Kierkegaard notes, is not distracted by the busy-ness of the world, nor does he submerge the thought of his own death; he challenges the notion that with death, all is over. He recognizes that earnestness about God begins this very day. Earnestness is the knowledge that one's death is certain while the lesson it teaches is the uncertainty of existence. These opposing rules of life, the certainty of death and the uncertainty of human expectations, are the earnest person's teachers, to which one must pay attention. The only question, says Kierkegaard, is whether the learner will pass the final examination.

Finally, as if to intensify and extend his reflections in *Purity*, and one of Geismar's favorite upbuilding discourses, "To Need God Is Man's Highest Perfection," Kierkegaard offers a series entitled *For Self-Examination* and *Judge for Yourself!* (cf. *TEK*, op. cit. p. 85). Written earlier, in 1851, these two clearly present a higher and preeminently religious mode of thought. Here as in *Sickness* and *Practice*, the ideality and provocative standards of religiousness "B," the Christian point of view, are upheld.

Kierkegaard returns in the first part of *For Self-Examination* with an allusion to the Socratic confession that at the age of seventy and shortly after being condemned innocently to death by hemlock poison, he is unable to be anything other than what he had always been. In the face of the urgings by his friends to go into exile rather than to die, Socrates refuses, knowing he would do the same in exile as he had done in Athens. In that case, by continuing to examine the opinions and presumptions of any person he chanced to meet, he would (note the irony) be guilty once more and deserving again of death.

Indirectly, the confession that he would not change is Kierkegaard's position also. He introduces the New Testament writer, James, whose well-known admonition is to be a "doer," not a hearer only of the message of Jesus. That is the need, says Søren Kierkegaard, to see oneself above all in the Scriptures as in a mirror, and to remember that it is "I" to whom they speak. So, this discourse in some respects is Kierkegaard's defense for his life and work, comparable to that of the Socratic confession.

In *Judge for Yourself!*, coupled with an additional but different treatment of the theme above, Kierkegaard presents a critique of the present Danish Church. Because Christ is the prototype of what it means to exist, one therefore cannot serve two masters, both human approval and Godly imitation. Unfortunately, Kierkegaard argues, imitation has been abolished in the Church, forsaken such that the committed individual will suffer in profound ways. We forget, he reminds the reader, that Jesus did not appear on earth to propose a doctrine; in reality his teaching, like that of Socrates, was his life, his very existence. And neither of them, despite their inexpressibly powerful witness to the truth, wrote anything at all!

However, Kierkegaard does pay homage to Martin Luther (1483-1546) and the sixteenth century Protestant Reformation for correcting abuses that had crept into the Church. In particular Luther refuted the view that personal salvation is humanly attainable by doing good works or by the purchase of indulgences, though perhaps well-meant, to lessen one's time in purgatory. On the basis of scriptural interpretation, Luther emphasized that faith alone can save a person for eternity. Nonetheless he also understood with James that striving always to do God's will as well as to hear it is essential to the task of imitating or, humanly speaking, embodying Jesus' witness to the world.

As I noted above, the foregoing characterizations of these various discourses, meditations, and deliberations are woefully inadequate and unfair to Kierkegaard; they do little or no justice to the poetic and dialectical penetration of the writings themselves. That can be corrected only by reading them—even, as Kierkegaard suggests elsewhere, out loud!

CONFLICT

Perhaps one can say that it was bound to happen. Satisfied with and justified by the completion of his plan for dual pseudonymous and named authorships, Kierkegaard could not long abide the critical reception the religious works, particularly *Practice in Christianity,* were met with from the Danish Church's leadership. Interpreters have spent a fair amount of effort to explain, if not always justify, Kierkegaard's final and so-called "attack on Christianity," though it is hardly necessary considering the high standards he set in his writings and with which he challenged the Church. Nonetheless, we should give some attention to how the conflict all began and then let the reader decide.

It began with an event that both saddened and disillusioned Kierkegaard when a person whose collegiality and close ties to the family he valued, died. It was none other than Bishop Mynster, head of the Danish Church. However, even preceding Mynster's death, Kierkegaard began to sense that the bishop did not share his published views that Christianity as represented in the Church did not live up to New Testament standards. To make matters worse, at the funeral the highly regarded Professor Martensen, Mynster's successor, virtually canonized his predecessor as one no less than the model of apostolic witness to Christianity's truth. In Kierkegaard's mind, this was not only unnecessarily glib in overlooking the less than admirable Mynster; it approached downright blasphemy.

Reflecting on this, Kierkegaard set out to write a series of articles that appeared in the newspaper *Faedrelandet* (The

Fatherland) in which he objected strongly to the eulogy. In addition, he published several subsequent pamphlets, virtually up to the period of his final illness and death, with the title *The Moment*, in which he reaffirmed the standards of New Testament Christianity—and, consistently, his own—in stark contrast to those of the present Church.

Unlike the indirect communication that marks the provocative and maieutic voices of his pseudonyms, Kierkegaard's new and final writings are uncompromisingly direct. Initially, of course, Kierkegaard's scorn for the presumption that Mynster was a model witness to the New Testament truth is directed at Martensen. Above all, Kierkegaard says in familiar ways, a witness to the truth suffers—not necessarily in physical terms, though existence has plenty of that. No, a truth-witness is initiated first and foremost "into interior struggles, into fear and trembling, into shuddering, into spiritual trials, into anxieties of soul, into torments of spirit, and then in addition [is] tried in all the sufferings that are more commonly talked about in the world" (*TEK*, op. cit., p. 426). It is the gist of Kierkegaard's concept of suffering. By implication, this kind of suffering has not been and is not now evident in the Church. As Kierkegaard sees the conflict, the model of human suffering is no less than that of Christ.

In subsequent pieces he consistently and pointedly raises the standards. Unlike Luther, he notes, who had ninety-five theses for reforming the Church, he himself has only one, and, moreover, nothing to reform: New Testament Christianity in the present Church does not exist at all!—and to preach otherwise is a crime or at least an untruth. He adamantly denies that he means to be a reformer in the tradition of Luther, least of all a prophet. He wants only one thing: "honesty," pure and simple. Even if the generation to which he belongs were to declare that it wants nothing to do with God or with a religion that can no longer speak to it with integrity, he would accept this judgment too, provided it were declared honestly before God. Indeed, Kierkegaard slyly notes, the standards are such that to be a Christian are rare, more extraordinary than to be a genius—and with that he proceeds to castigate the Church for, in his penetrating judgment, its fundamental lack of honesty.

Again, Kierkegaard vehemently denies that he himself has lived up to the standards about which he has written, and the last thing he wants is to be identified with other critics who may question the Church's stand on one issue or another. All he insists is that what the present Church represents is not the truth, and definitely not the truth embodied in Christ. He notes how in his own life he was brought little by little to the questions of what it takes, what it means to be a Christian, why he should be careful not to take offense, why the collisions one experiences in one's inner self must be such as even to hate one's family—collisions that permeate the New Testament. He now believes that those collisions are there "because Christianity knows very well that to become a Christian is to become, humanly speaking, unhappy in this life, yet blessedly awaiting an eternal happiness. [God] makes you unhappy, but he does it out of love; blessed is the one who is not offended!" (*Ibid.*, p. 437).

Shortly after this writing appeared, he collapsed in the company of friends. As they tried to help him up, he wryly objected, saying, in effect: "Don't bother; just have someone sweep this thing off the floor."

POSTSCRIPT

There is perhaps little if anything more that in such a brief but perhaps seductive overview of Søren Kierkegaard's life and writings must be said. The brevity stands in stark contrast to his prodigious and provocative authorship during a very short life; the seduction lies in the hope that this modest effort will entice the reader to discover in Kierkegaard what is not abridged.

Nonetheless, there remain several important writings of Kierkegaard about which regretfully I have not told you. For example, *The Point of View for My Work As an Author* is often overlooked, though clearly something of a fine spiritual autobiography. Another is Kierkegaard's final published meditation, *The Changelessness of God*, which appeared just weeks before his death. It should be ranked among his best. But because *Point of View* represents a final apology or defense of his authorship, I should offer some sense of it, though it may not tell you much more than you already know from the foregoing.

In an early explanation Kierkegaard concedes that he is a self-published "poet" whose literary efforts may or may not gain a large or admiring readership in a small country like Denmark; after all, he is most devoted to the "single, individual reader." Nonetheless the work is important and purposeful, and he reaffirms its principal line of thought from the esthetic and ethical up to *The Postscript*, though the pseudonym Anti-Climacus and his two later writings, *Sickness* and *Practice*, in fact mark the end of these works.

Above all he insists that as a whole the entire authorship has "religious awareness" as its goal, and that (re: *Purity of Heart*) he has "willed only one thing": ultimately to represent Christianity in its most vital form. His writings, he says, develop a line of reasoning from the complex to the simple, from philosophical and poetic reflections to something relatively easy to understand, from indirect communication designed to lure the reader into the truth, and finally to a communication meant to offer the truth directly.

Kierkegaard goes on in great detail to provide the rationale by which the dual authorship arrives at a point where the initial appeal to the public is reduced finally to an earnest interest in "the solitary individual" and one's personal relationship to God. He insists that his entire named authorship was intentionally dedicated to that "existing individual" reader, and the whole idea, though he grants it is "unauthorized," is to make that reader aware of the religious.

In subsequent reflections Kierkegaard argues that he has done this in large part because the term, Christendom, is an illusion—that there are very few true Christians (a quality he himself does not claim), that religion is not just something one should get serious about only in old age, leaving the esthetic life behind. The religious life is eternally valid, and the person who deludes oneself into thinking otherwise must free oneself of this confusion and earnestly understand what is at stake. That is the sole purpose of the authorship.

In the process, however, Kierkegaard confesses to a charade, that is, of personally assuming at first and in public the esthetic stance (like that of "the young man"?) as he roamed the streets of Copenhagen. This was intentional for identifying with the popular culture, the Danish way of life. It was to seduce readers indirectly and gradually into the subsequent authorship, the work that ultimately revealed his true character and purpose.

He explains at great length why this was a necessary irony, and why at the publication of *The Postscript* he felt it timely to reveal his responsibility for the entire authorship(s). The timing was to insure that, after all, his purpose was a highly serious one which he had underscored with the parallel publication of *Edifying Discourses, Works of Love*, and many others under his own name. As it turned out, however, he began to feel the decision to bring to an end his pseudonymous work (*The Postscript*) was, for the sake of his ultimate plan, too abrupt or premature. Thus, he wrote additional works like *Practice in Christianity*, in which he reclaimed the use of indirect communication together with the pseudonym Anti-Climacus, but now he added his own name as editor, responsible for its publication.

In general, this lengthy explanation for a profoundly developed authorship accords with our preceding descriptions of Kierkegaard's life and works. Still, we might end this as David and Lillian Swenson did by quoting Kierkegaard's words from *The Point of View*, a substantial work published in part in 1851, but fully only after his death. It is clearly an indication that he has seen himself also as something of a martyr for the truth:

> When my poet comes he will assign me a place among those who have suffered for an idea; he will say about me: "The martyrdom which this author suffered was due to the fact that he was a genius living in a market town. In Eternity it will be his comfort that he has suffered voluntarily, and has not supported his cause by the help of any illusion or concealed himself behind any illusion. His sufferings have been a prudently pious gathering together of savings for Eternity: there he has the memory that he was faithful to himself and to his first love, with which he has loved all those who have suffered in the world. The dialectical structure that he erected, he

could not dedicate to any human being, much less to himself. If he should dedicate it to anyone, it would have to be to Providence, to whom, indeed, it was consecrated, day after day, year after year, by the author, who, to speak historically, died of a mortal disease, but, to speak poetically, died of a longing for Eternity, where he desires nothing better than that he might there uninterruptedly give thanks unto God" (Swenson, op. cit., p. xxi).

AFTERTHOUGHTS

There may be a few points from previous sections that bear repeating:

First: We have learned that *despair* is the predominant human condition, the "sickness unto death" that if unrecognized in the self is nonetheless latent in unexamined, unawakened innocence and ignorance. If despair is once recognized, however, the sickness of the self can, by virtue of its personal acceptance, begin to be healed. Despair is an unwillingness initially to understand and to be oneself, though once self-consciously recognized, is also the possibility, the occasion to will to be oneself. Fortified by free will, despair presents itself as a decisive threshold between the esthetic and ethical dimensions of existence—a threshold that ironically trades one form of despair for another against the impossible demands of the ethical highest good. It is a condition, a disability ultimately relieved—healed—only by divine or supernatural intervention based on one's eternal validity or link to God. But to believe that one can be free of despair by an act of will is a futile misreading of the self and its capacity.

Second: We have learned that *self-knowledge* as practiced by Socrates is, humanly speaking, the highest form of understanding. It reflects the paradox that to be wise is to recognize one's ignorance and that truth is achieved through rigorous self-examination, inwardly, immanently. Still, this truth falls short of the final truth, the Truth conveyed from without and transcendently by God. Socratic ignorance makes clear that there is a qualitative difference between these truths. Human truth is otherwise subject to the self's potential for misjudgment and despair. Even so, self-awareness captures the truth of real existence subjectively, not objectively; existence is understood in inwardness.

Third: The climax of despair is reached in the experience of *suffering*, not just that common to human life but also through the sickness unto death in knowing that even the most ethical or immanently religious position cannot bring about lasting peace of mind, well-being, or happiness. The paradoxical pattern for the ultimate in suffering is that of the incarnate God who suffered the ignominy of rejection and crucifixion, the epitome of human offense. This God allowed as the means to transform the human condition from the waywardly meaningless to the potentially meaningful, from the offense known to reason to the paradox of faith, and from lingering despair to eternal happiness.

Fourth: Kierkegaard learned a great deal from Socrates whose maieutic method of self-examination he clearly adopted as a *dialectical* style. Kierkegaard assigned Socratic ignorance to the self as a state embracing despair. He recognized Socrates' argument for recollection as the immanent search for truth by inference and deduction, and he saw in Socratic irony an element of the paradox, the inability by reason alone to achieve the ethical ideal. Kierkegaard thoroughly appreciated and utilized the Platonic dialogues in which Socrates is portrayed, and he created a dialogue-like style to engage and indirectly communicate with the reader. And, toward the end of his life and subjected to the vicious attacks on his authorship, Kierkegaard assumed the legendary stance of Socrates awaiting unwarranted death by hemlock: he made it clear that his detractors, after all his years of saying the same and the same, could hardly expect him to change his unpopular ways now. Indeed, in one issue of *The Moment* he plaintively longed to be able to speak—just a half hour—with Socrates.

Fifth: Kierkegaard perceived in human existence crucial outlooks presented both pseudonymously in embodied characters and personally under his own name through complementary authorships. He discerned the human condition in terms of *stages*, a spectrum of existential dimensions: esthetic, ironic, ethical, humorous, immanent and transcendent religiousness. All occupy to a relative or potential extent the existing person such that to be ethical, for example, does not eliminate the esthetic but only takes precedence over it by a greater passion, a greater love, to will the good. In the end, the greatest passion is faith, "out over 70,000 fathoms," in the face of the offensiveness it makes to good sense.

To these existential dimensions Kierkegaard added the human experiences of doubt, anxiety, fear, resignation, love—despair, of course—and all the various presentiments that qualify, define and hyphenate the self from time to time. Intermittently they are the governing moods, the dominant emotions, the passions and real life situations we encounter, the inner environment in which we live, move, and have our being.

Finally: The predominant focus of Søren Kierkegaard's discourse literature is to awaken the individual reader to an *awareness* of the condition and lingering concerns of the self-conscious mind. The discourses probe in a searching, dialectical manner some of the most nagging of one's innermost thoughts and emotions—unspoken questions for which the reader has no decisive answers: What, I wonder, should I make of the widespread reliance on the supernatural? Is there any real relief for the anxieties and despair I so often seem to suffer? What after all are the chances for a lasting love when broken relationships are so common? Is there any percentage in doing the right thing, when doing so seems naïve and contrary to the behavior of many? How is happiness possible, and how is it sustained, when it seems so limited and fleeting from day to day? How can it possibly make sense that a man was God, or that God was a man, when the whole idea is so offensive to a thoughtful person?

What Kierkegaard offers, indirectly, are three principal options that pervade in varying measure the human condition, though only one of which can be personally appropriated as one's governing passion: I can avoid the distasteful, the painful, and pursue what promises to be esthetically pleasurable; I can strive consistently to do the right thing, to be ethical; or I can have faith in a loving, forgiving God whose incarnate human life I am supposed to imitate. Which will it be?

There you have it: a beginning, a glimpse, a footnote, a very brief overview of the life and writings of Søren Kierkegaard. Read him!

ACKNOWLEDGMENTS

I am particularly grateful for the critical comments from those whose personal achievements as well as uncommon familiarity with Kierkegaard have greatly improved this modest effort. They include Paul Sponheim, David Preus, Lloyd Svendsbye, Marilyn Preus, Renee Hermanson, and Leonard Flachman. Though unintended, any errors and oversights are mine.

PERTINENT DATES AND FACTS ABOUT KIERKEGAARD

1813	Born May 5, 1813, Copenhagen, Denmark, the youngest child of Michael Pedersen Kierkegaard, successful hosiery merchant who retires early and home-schools Soren in classical language and literature in hopes he would one day enter the ministry.
1831	Enters the University of Copenhagen and over a ten-year period studies literature, history, philosophy, and classics
1837	Meets the sixteen-year-old Regine Olsen, daughter of a prominent Copenhagen family; later proposes marriage, but in 1841 breaks off the engagement.
1838	Michael Pedersen dies during Soren's theological studies to enter the ministry in the Danish Church.
1841	Completes university work with the terminal degree for a dissertation on *The Concept of Irony, With Continual Reference to Socrates*.
1841	Travels to Berlin to attend lectures and there begins to write and develop a dual authorship plan, with some works to appear under assumed names and others under his own name (see below).
1842-43	Writes but does not publish *Johannes Climacus, or De omnibus dubitandum est*.

1843	*Either/Or* edited by Victor Eremita.
1843-44	The *Edifying Discourses* by S. Kierkegaard.
1843	*Fear and Trembling* by Johannes de Silentio.
1843	*Repetition* by Constantine Constantius.
1844	*Philosophical Fragments* by Johannes Climacus.
1844	*The Concept of Anxiety* by Vigilius Haufniensis.
1845	*Thoughts on Crucial Situations in Human Life* by S. Kierkegaard.
1845	*Stages on Life's Way* by Hilarius Bookbinder.
1846	*Concluding Unscientific Postscript to the Philosophical Fragments* by Johannes Climacus.
1847	A series of attacks on Kierkegaard appear in "The Corsair," a local paper.
1847	*Purity of Heart Is to Will One Thing* by S. Kierkegaard.
1847	*The Gospel of Suffering* and *The Lily of the Field and the Bird of the Air* by S. Kierkegaard.
1847	*Works of Love* by S. Kierkegaard.
1848-49	*Christian Discourses* and three discourses to prepare for holy communion, by S. Kierkegaard.
1849	*The Sickness Unto Death* by Anti-Climacus, edited by S. Kierkegaard.
1850	*Practice in Christianity* by Anti-Climacus, edited by S. Kierkegaard.
1851	(and from 1848) *The Point of View for My Work As an Author*, by S. Kierkegaard, published in 1859.
1851-52	Discourses on *For Self-Examination* and *Judge for Yourself!* by S. Kierkegaard.

1854	The death of Bishop Mynster and his successor's (Martensen) encomium on Mynster's witness.
1854-55	Kierkegaard's critical "Faedrelandet" articles and "The Moment" pamphlets.
1855	Kierkegaard's final work, *The Changelessness of God*.
1855	Kierkegaard's death, in November.

CHRONOLOGY OF RELEVANT HISTORICAL FIGURES

Lao-tse (or Lao Tzu; 604-31 B.C.)
Popular Chinese teacher whose philosophy of life, The Way, is found in various editions of the *Tao Te Ching*.

Confucius (551-479 B.C.)
Legendary Chinese philosopher much of whose thought is collected in the *I Ching*, the Book of Change.

Socrates (460-399 B.C.)
Prominent and controversial thinker in Athens, Greece; likened to a midwife whose manner of questioning conventional wisdom gave birth to truthful insight; taught Plato but wrote nothing.

Plato (429-347 B.C.)
Athenian philosopher, pupil of Socrates, famous for writing *The Dialogues of Plato* which portrays Socrates and promulgates his own views, especially in dialogues *The Symposium* and *The Republic*.

Aristotle (384-322 B.C.)
Pupil of Plato, responsible for writing or collecting the knowledge of his day; taught Alexander the Great and wrote the well-known work *Nicomachean Ethics* as well as other major works on various topics.

Jesus (ca. 4 B.C.- ca. 30 A.D.)
Native of Israel, influential reformer and teacher, source of the Christian religion; wrote nothing, but his followers recorded his life and teachings in the New Testament scriptures of the Bible.

St. Anselm (1033-1109)
Archbishop of Canterbury, England, famous for his writings *The Proslogion* and *The Monologion* which develop well-reasoned proofs for the existence of God.

Martin Luther (1483-1546)
German theologian and religious reformer, Bible translator, and prime mover of the Protestant Reformation.

Rene Descartes (1596-1650)
Brilliant French mathematician and philosopher who in his *Discourses* turned the idea of doubt into the principle of rationality; called the Father of Rationalism.

Blaise Pascal (1623-1662)
French philosopher noted for his written meditations or *Pensees* that also incorporate an interesting argument for ethico-religious faith whether or not God exists.

John Locke (1632-1704)
English statesman and philosopher of perception whose treatises on civil government and liberty influenced early American leaders to write the Declaration of Independence, and whose insights into the nature of knowledge were widely accepted.

Immanuel Kant (1724-1804)
German, considered by many to be one of the greatest philosophers of all time for his theory of knowledge, *The Critique of Pure Reason:* experience is possible due to an unseen reality that one must infer; also wrote on ethics, *Groundwork of the Metaphysics of Morals*: if there is a moral order in reality, it has the nature of a universal law, an imperative for all.

Johann Georg Hamann (1730-1788)
German mystic, critic of Kant, wrote *Socratic Memorabilia*, a profound but oblique development of Christian faith as reflected in the figure of Socrates.

G. W. F. Hegel (1770-1831)
German philosopher, wrote monumental works ranging speculatively over philosophy and world history in an attempt to provide a unified theory of reality and cosmic change; Kierkegaard, a contemporary, disputed the attempt.

John Stuart Mill (1806-1873)
English statesman and philosopher, popular for his view of ethics (opposed to Kant), believed that the highest good is happiness defined as more pleasure than pain for most people most of the time.

Søren Kierkegaard (1813-1855)
Danish philosopher-theologian, devotee of Socrates, critical of Hegel for slighting the importance of lived existence and the human condition.

Jean-Paul Sartre (1905-1980)
French writer and philosopher, famous for making Existentialism prominent; wrote *Being and Nothingness*; admired Kierkegaard's work.

Albert Camus (1913-1960)
A popular French writer and existentialist philosopher whose writings include *The Stranger* and *The Plague*.

INDEX

A
"A" religiousness 61, 62, 63, 67, 80, 81
Abraham 14, 20, 45, 48, 49, 58, 65
Afham, William 28
Anselm, St. 57, 102
Anti-Climacus 20, 47, 48, 49, 56, 62, 63, 64, 65, 66, 67, 69, 89, 97, 99
Anxiety 20, 40, 41, 43, 44, 47, 50, 95
Aristophanes 15, 30
Aristotle 38, 54, 80, 101
attack on Christianity 86
authorship 12, 15, 17, 20, 21, 22, 34, 38, 44, 54, 61, 68, 69, 75, 80, 86, 89, 90, 91, 94, 95

B
"B" religiousness 61, 62, 63, 67, 79, 80, 82, 84
Bentham, Jeremy 22
Bookbinder, Hilarius 20, 26, 28, 30, 99

C
Camus, Albert 38, 103
change 26, 35, 36, 40, 53, 57, 67, 69, 72, 75, 76, 77, 78, 80, 82, 84, 89, 94, 98, 100
Changelessness of God, The 89, 100
Christian Discourses 75, 78, 99
Climacus, Johannes 20, 42, 45, 51, 54, 59, 61, 63, 80, 98, 99
Concept of Anxiety, The 20, 43, 47, 99
Concept of Irony, The 15, 16, 21, 49, 63, 98
Concluding Unscientific Postscript, The 20, 51, 54, 99
consciousness of God 81, 82
consciousness of sin 67, 68, 79
conflict 27, 67, 75, 86, 87
Confucius 38, 101
Constantius, Constantine 20, 31, 99
Corsair 75, 99

D
deliberation, discourses for 41, 76, 78, 85
Descartes, Rene 25, 27, 38, 42, 45, 102
de Silentio, Johannes 20, 45, 56, 99
despair 8, 10, 14, 24, 25, 26, 37, 38, 40, 41, 42, 43, 44, 46, 47, 48, 49, 50, 55, 60, 61, 62, 67, 71, 77, 78, 79, 81, 82, 93, 94, 95
dialectical 13, 19, 41, 72, 76, 85, 91, 94, 95
Dialogues of Plato 12, 39, 101
Diotima, the seer 28, 29, 39
doubt 23, 25, 26, 40, 41, 42, 43, 46, 50, 95, 99

E
earnestness 83
Edifying Discourses 21, 69, 70, 72, 75, 91, 99
Either/Or 20, 21, 24, 25, 27, 31, 33, 41, 82

Eremita, Victor 20, 21, 31, 98
esthetic 8, 22, 23, 24, 25, 26, 27, 28, 31, 32, 33, 34, 35, 44, 45, 47, 60, 63, 76, 80, 82, 89, 90, 93, 95, 96
eternal validity 25, 29, 49, 60, 70, 79, 93
ethical 22, 23, 24, 27, 28, 32, 34, 35, 37, 41, 44, 45, 46, 47, 55, 56, 60, 63, 69, 70, 72, 74, 78, 80, 82, 89, 93, 94, 95, 96
ethico-religious 52, 54, 69, 72, 73, 75, 76, 99
Euthyphro 13
Existentialism 38, 44, 100

F

faith 8, 23, 27, 28, 33, 36, 46, 47, 58, 64, 67, 70, 71, 78, 79, 82, 83, 85, 91, 94, 95, 96, 99
Fashion Designer, the 33, 34
Fear and Trembling 20, 45, 56, 58, 62, 74, 99
Faedrelandet 86, 100
For Self-Examination 21, 84, 99

G

Geismar, Eduard 9, 55, 56
God, consciousness of 81, 82
God-man 64, 66
Gospel of Suffering, The 99
guilt, consciousness of 62, 67

H

Hamann, Johann Georg 39, 102
Haufniensis, Vigilius 43, 47, 99
Hegel, G. W. F. 16, 40, 48, 103
Hong, Howard and Edna 5, 9, 10, 17
humor 27, 60, 63, 95

I

ignorance 16, 29, 33, 43, 44, 47, 52, 58, 63, 93, 94
"In Vino Veritas" 28, 30, 31, 34

indirect communication 20, 34, 87, 90, 91
innocence 33, 35, 43, 44, 47, 93
irony 15, 16, 21, 27, 34, 40, 49, 60, 63, 75, 84, 91, 94

J

Jesus 53, 62, 64, 70, 71, 72, 74, 76, 78, 84, 85, 101
Job 35, 36, 44, 46, 62
Judge For Yourself! 21, 84, 99
Judge William 22, 26, 27, 29, 37, 41, 44, 45, 47, 48, 82

K

Kant, Immanuel 16, 22, 45, 102
Kierkegaard, Michael Pedersen 12, 98
Kierkegaard, Soren Aabye 1, 2, 4, 5, 7, 8, 9, 10, 11, 12, 14, 15, 16, 17, 18, 19, 20, 21, 22, 23, 25, 26, 27, 28, 30, 32, 34, 36, 37, 38, 39, 40, 41, 42, 43, 44, 45, 49, 51, 54, 56, 57, 59, 60, 61, 62, 63, 64, 66, 68, 69, 70, 71, 72, 73, 74, 75, 76, 77, 78, 79, 80, 81, 82, 83, 84, 85, 86, 87, 88, 89, 90, 91, 94, 95, 96, 97, 99, 100, 103

L

Lao-tse 38, 101
left hand authorship 20, 21
Locke, John 50, 102
love 13, 17, 18, 21, 28, 29, 30, 31, 32, 33, 50, 53, 65, 75, 76, 77, 78, 80, 82, 88, 91, 95
Luther, Martin 85, 102

M

maieutic (see midwifery) 20, 52, 74, 87, 94
Martensen, Professor 86, 100
Meno 51

midwifery (see maieutic) 20, 52, 74, 87, 94
Mill, John Stuart 22, 45, 103
Moment, The 100
Mynster, Bishop 86, 100

N
Newton, Isaac 38
Nichomachean Ethics 55, 101

O
objectivity 50, 51, 55, 57
offense 64, 65, 66, 67, 88, 94
Olson, Regine 18, 98

P
paradox 27, 35, 46, 56, 58, 59, 64, 65, 70, 93, 94
Pascal, Blaise 57, 102
Paul, the apostle 36, 38, 45, 77, 97, 100
Philosophical Fragments 20, 39, 51, 54, 99
philosophy of life 38, 98
Plato 12, 13, 15, 28, 29, 32, 33, 38, 39, 40, 51, 52, 53, 54, 73, 76, 78, 94, 101
Point of View for My Work As An Author, The 89, 99
Practice in Christianity 20, 63, 82, 86, 91, 99
Purity of Heart 72, 90, 99

R
recollection 28, 52, 62, 94
religiousness 60, 61, 62, 63, 67, 79, 80, 81, 82, 84, 95
Repetition 20, 31, 34, 44, 56, 62, 67, 99

S
Sartre, Jean-Paul 38, 103
Seducer, The 30, 31, 33, 34, 37
seeker, the 81, 82

self 7, 8, 11, 12, 13, 14, 15, 16, 17, 18, 19, 20, 21, 22, 24, 25, 26, 29, 33, 34, 35, 36, 37, 39, 40, 41, 42, 43, 44, 45, 46, 47, 48, 49, 50, 51, 52, 53, 54, 55, 56, 57, 58, 60, 62, 63, 65, 66, 67, 68, 70, 71, 72, 73, 74, 75, 76, 77, 78, 79, 80, 81, 82, 84, 87, 88, 89, 90, 91, 92, 93, 94, 95
self-knowledge 39, 44, 72, 93
Sickness Unto Death 20, 47, 63, 99
Socrates 12, 13, 15, 16, 17, 20, 28, 29, 30, 38, 39, 41, 43, 51, 52, 53, 58, 59, 60, 61, 62, 63, 84, 85, 93, 94, 102, 103, 104
Spinoza, Baruch 80
spirit 27, 29, 36, 37, 41, 43, 44, 47, 48, 60, 87, 89
Stages on Life's Way 3, 20, 26, 27, 28, 30, 37, 44, 52, 73, 76, 99
stages 19, 22, 27, 37, 60, 95
subjectivity 8, 15, 49, 50, 55, 57, 58, 59
suffering 18, 35, 44, 56, 61, 65, 66, 69, 70, 71, 72, 74, 77, 78, 79, 80, 87, 91, 94
Swenson, David F. and Lillian 75
Symposium, The 28, 98
synthesis 47, 48, 56, 60

T
Thomte, Reidar 5, 9, 32, 54
Thoughts on Crucial Situations in Human Life 80, 99
truth 8, 16, 17, 20, 30, 44, 50, 51, 52, 53, 54, 57, 58, 59, 62, 64, 66, 72, 76, 77, 85, 86, 87, 88, 90, 91, 93, 94, 98

U
upbuilding, edifying discourses 21, 69, 74, 76, 77, 84

W

Works of Love, The 21, 75, 76, 78, 82, 91, 99

Y

"young man," the 22, 23, 24, 25, 26, 32, 34, 35, 36, 37, 41, 42, 43, 44, 47, 90

www.ingramcontent.com/pod-product-compliance
Lightning Source LLC
Chambersburg PA
CBHW071216070526
44584CB00019B/3044